I0521518

UNMASKING THE REAL ME

Tatyana M. Ferrer

Book Cover Design: Ahsan Hunter

Printed by: Prize Publishing House, LLC in the United States of America.

First printing edition 2022.

Prize Publishing House
P.O. Box 9856, Chesapeake, VA 23321
www.PrizePublishingHouse.com

ISBN (Paperback): 979-8-9858926-5-9
ISBN (E-Book): 979-8-9858926-6-6

Library of Congress Control Number: 2022909430

CONTENTS

ACKNOWLEDGMENTS

I have always loved writing ever since I discovered what writing was and the power of writing my thoughts and experiences. At the age of thirteen, when I gave my life to Jesus Christ, I began writing poems and sermonettes. My former bishop, my grandfather, also pushed the youth to be active in the church. I thank my grandfather and Bishop Samuel S. Simms, who passed away in 2012 from colon cancer, for being great men and leaders in my life and investing so much in me.

To my parents, Robert and Sherell Ferrer, who were the youth leaders at the church I grew up in. To the current pastor and first lady of the church I attend, Faith Family Church, for always encouraging all the youth, including my siblings and I, to work in ministry and love God with all of our hearts, and their six children, Davante, Briana, Imani, Aniaya, Asia and I, to be active in the church by singing, ushering, acting in skits, reciting a poem or even preaching sermonettes. The last three, Savanna, Faith, and Ethan, came later down the line. We all were taught things about God as well. Specifically Jesus Christ and the importance of having him in their lives. I thank my parents for being a positive influence and for teaching all eight of us about Jesus Christ. For sharing wisdom with us and being great examples. They lived the Christian lifestyle in front of us so that we would be inspired by it. My relationship with God was truly inspired by their relationships with God. I do not want to solely focus on spirituality without sharing my point of view on life and my experiences.

1

Writing is My Therapy

In everyday life, writing is needed for different things. Whether to release negative energy, take note of important things we have to do, keep memories, or even a collection of all of the above. Writing is therapeutic for me. I find myself writing a lot for courses in college, sermons for church, and poetry. However, I have never gotten the opportunity to share how I really feel about being a young Christian. I have read many books on Christianity and how to walk a life honorable to God. But, I have only read these books from an older Christian perspective. I have not read a Christian book from a young Christian's perspective. Today, we endure a lot of temptation where laws and views are changing, and people in our generation are pursuing the things of the word. I want to

1

write this book to share my views on current issues, struggles, and how to stand firm as a Christian. So many people believe that young people don't go through anything in life simply because of age. The truth is that we go through a lot of storms. We don't speak about storms because of shame or just feeling like others will not understand. I have learned a lot about myself, life, and other people in these 22 years.

I received Jesus Christ and became a Christian at thirteen years old. Not only did I begin the Christian walk at thirteen, but I also began the work of a disciple as well. I spoke messages, wrote poetry, and sang songs at that young age, doing whatever was needed from me. I was genuinely excited about the journey when the journey first began. It's like a menstrual cycle. A young girl is excited about growing into a woman until she realizes the pain and suffering she has to endure just because she is a woman. I didn't know the pain and the suffering I would have to go through as a Christian until I went through it. I was unfortunately unaware of the side effects that would occur as a young girl proclaiming Jesus Christ as her savior and king. One side effect was that I couldn't fit in. No matter how hard I tried, I would be that quiet, smart girl and "teacher's pet" who was there to help with assignments.

Many times I just felt misunderstood by people. The loneliness that I was feeling did cause me to experience depression, suicidal thoughts, and addiction, and ultimately destroyed my relationship with other people. Isn't that strange? How can one's loneliness destroy the relationship they do have? The answer to that question is unforgiveness. Unforgiveness caused me to push people away. I did not want the people who wanted me to want me. I did not want to let people get to know me. I didn't want people to get to know me because of the bad relationships I had with people in my past. I was too afraid of being hurt again. It was also the very thing that encouraged my struggle with watching pornography to continue. And of course, I don't blame myself for all of my psychological and emotional struggles because one should never blame themselves for hurt or pain caused by another person's actions. But one thing I do know is that forgiveness is for you and not for the other person. Changing is for you. Freedom is for you. Your physical health is better when you heal and forgive. Your psychological and emotional health is so much better when you forgive.

For too long, I have been caught up with being focused on being a better person so that others can like me. Even in writing this book, I was so concerned about how others would people perceive me after sharing what I shared? *"Is my positive reputation going to diminish? What if people who looked at me as a role model or positive influence change their thought about me?"* These unimportant questions ran through my head to keep me from writing this book. Fortunately, I no longer care about what others will think about me and who they think I should be. Now, I'm just focused on being the best me for me.

In this book, I will expose myself, share my thoughts and experiences, give a true insight into the life of a believer, and be honest about some of the struggles. I want to let everyone

3

know through my life that being a Christian and living in righteousness is not easy, but it's worth it. After you've said that first, "yes," there are plenty of times you'll ask God why and question that yes. But, in the end, everything will work together for those who truly love God.

God uses the good and the bad in our lives to create a masterpiece. I am aware that it won't be easy to share my experiences. However, I promised myself and God that I would share everything that needed to be shared. Writing this book is helping to set me free as I release the ugly truth. I'm sharing my story to help you know that you are not alone. I understand your pain, and I understand your struggle. My prayer is that this book encourages you to keep your faith and never lose hope in yourself or God. You can be free from anything that is holding you down. This includes being free from the opinions of others and focusing more on your freedom than your reputation.

2

Who is Tatyana Monae Ferrer?

I found it a little challenging to begin this book. However, I think the best way to start is by introducing myself. I am Tatyana Monae Ferrer. I am 22 years young. I have eight siblings – six younger sisters, a younger brother, and an older brother. My parents, Robert and Sherell Ferrer, raised us in a two-parent home. Not only that, but they raised us in a household where they were committed to each other in marriage and to God. We all were raised to fear God. However, as I know now, although the same parents may have raised you with the same values, rules, and perspectives as your siblings, each one may choose to have a different perception

5

of that advice. Or maybe each person applies it differently to their lives. Don't get me wrong, all of my siblings have some acknowledgment of God in their life. However, I have been known to be more public by teaching and preaching the gospel to my peers.

It's kind of crazy because my personality is what you call an ambivert. I am primarily an introvert, but the extrovert side comes out at work and when I'm speaking publicly. An ambivert is "a <u>person</u> who has <u>features</u> of both an <u>introvert</u> (= someone who <u>prefers</u> to <u>spend</u> <u>time</u> <u>alone</u>) and an <u>extrovert</u> (= someone who <u>prefers</u> to be with other <u>people</u>) in <u>their</u> <u>personality</u>" (Dictionary.Cambridge.org, 2022). I never knew this terminology until I looked it up. I recognized that I am primarily an introvert. But, I can also be an extrovert in the right space and when I feel comfortable. However, I cherish my alone time. Even with so many siblings, I have always had this independent mindset. This has served me well because it helps me be a good leader. I, unfortunately, had a supervisor question my introverted behavior. She specifically asked, "How do you think your personality fits the field of social work?" This was a whole roasting session about my personality. We were supposed to be talking about how we were supposed to report to her and a different supervisor because my supervisor had left. She then asked whether I was comfortable there and being in the social work field. I responded that I was. Then she stated, "People in the office think you're really quiet, and I noticed that when we went to the going away breakfast." I'm explaining to her that

I say good morning to everyone in the morning. I may be to myself, but I make sure my work gets done. Then she stated, "Yes, I see the hard work, and thank you for working so hard." The real reason was that the people I worked with were not my cup of tea. They would talk about drinking all the time and other things that I'm not interested in. That doesn't make me awkward or not a good fit for social work. I may be cordial with them and talk about work stuff. However, I have no need or desire to be buddies with certain people. It is biblical to be different from everyone and separate yourself from certain things.

Psalm 1:1, KJV states, "Blessed is the man that walketh not in the counsel of the ungodly, nor standeth in the way of sinners, nor sitteth in the seat of the scornful." (KJV) If we link up to unbelievers as Christians, we can become contaminated with negativity, gossip, depression, and dark spirits. All of these things and bad company corrupt good morals. I am all for ministering to the lost souls. Also, I know we positively influence people who don't know Christ. And I am all for not judging someone when they are unaware that what they are doing is wrong. However, I would never allow negative influences in my life. So, throughout the conversation, I explained to her that my quietness is necessary and spelled out how it has helped me in my career. The thing is, I always get the work done. So, I reminded myself about God and how He works. You may not have the "right" personality for a job. But, if you're anointed, you're anointed. I've succeeded at things on my job that my co-workers could not succeed at. They'll come to me and ask me how I did it. And I'll give them the tips because I'm not a mean person. I like helping people.

I briefly questioned my passion for social work because of being told that I didn't have the right personality. However, I reminded myself of all the things I've experienced and the path that led me to this career. I have been the president of a Christian club at college and spoke about Jesus Christ and salvation at many churches. I only mention this because this was a part of my challenge of being the older sister, saved, and always meant to be the role model. I'm not going to lie; this placed some pressure on me because I was the oldest and had publicly received Christ.

There is also an unspoken expectation or challenge that comes with being the "poster Christian girl." On many occasions, I felt lonely and out of place. I felt this at home and everywhere I went. With my sisters mostly because we lived with each other. Because we were different and valued different things, I didn't feel close to them. I wanted to feel like a part. But, I recognized that our different personalities and different views clashed. Although I understand that our personalities clash, I recognize there is beauty in our differences. I will speak about how my relationship with my siblings at the beginning relates to my social life later on.

I also want to acknowledge my baby brother R.J who passed away at a very young age. Unfortunately, he struggled with a rare disease known as Pompe. He never got to experience life to its fullest. But, as his family, we made it the best that we could

8

by loving and caring for him. I took his loss personally for a long time because of how it happened. I remember the many times that we had to rush him to the hospital because he could not breathe. In those moments, I knew my dad did not want to get a ticket for driving above the speed limit or breaking the rules of driving. But, all he was focused on was saving his son's life and relieving him from the pain.

Through those years, I knew my parents were struggling to keep it together mentally and emotionally. But, they always kept it together for us. That's a major sacrifice that I will always appreciate them for – for not allowing tragedies to destroy the family and always making sure they were there for us as much as they could be. There were times when his breathing machine wasn't working properly. My parents would have to go through so many obstacles to get it fixed. I remember only one time when my dad broke down in front of me about my brother RJ. That was the morning he died. He came into my room early in the morning. This was kind of weird because it was so early. His face looked sad, and he sat close to me on my bed and started touching me. He said, "RJ is gone." When he said it, I didn't believe it, or I didn't want to believe it. I said, "Are you serious?" He said, "Yes. He's gone. But it's okay. He's in a better place." After the information set in, I just poured my eyes out, crying. Then my dad just started crying with me. I barely see him cry, so that's how I knew this was real.

After I left the room, some of my family members came to the house to check up on us. Some of my sisters and I couldn't be at the house anymore because RJ had passed away there. So, my grandfather came over to the house and consoled us. He also decided to take us to his house, which was good because it helped us cope better. I would say it definitely helped me the most because I went through a stage of guilt due to his loss. I happened to be the last person with him the night before. He was playing with me, and his machine was not acting weird at the time. So, in my young mind, I thought that maybe if I stayed awake with him a little longer to alert someone that his machine was not working, he would still be alive. But, now, as I have become wiser, I know that God's will always takes place whether we are ready for it or not. Regardless of if we want our loved ones gone or not. God has the final say in everything. And I have learned from my mom that when someone is sick, pray for God's will to be done.

After losing my baby brother to this disease, I lost my grandfather (mom's dad), who was the bishop of the church I grew up in. His life impacted his church members, sons, daughters, grandchildren, and neighborhood. My grandfather was one person who positively influenced anyone, whether they were someone he knew or just met. Knowing how much positivity he poured into people makes me want to be that positive role model that my heart, spirit, and soul want me to be. But, I know that everyone has flaws, and my imperfections don't prevent me from positively influencing people. At least it shouldn't. I actually surrendered my life to Jesus Christ under his ministry, which was really special to me.

I received Christ at thirteen years old. This was really special to me because I was always able to go to him as a grandfather and, at the time, my pastor for spiritual advice. I was a new Christian around the time that he passed away. So, his death impacted me from two perspectives. One being a grandfather and another being a spiritual advisor. He was truly the rock of the family. These two deaths impacted me deeply. Losing my grandpa and brother at this point in my life was devastating to my family and me. Fortunately, I was able to turn to my parents when I was going through a tough time with it. But, losing a loved one never becomes easy to deal with. I always think about it. I always think about the day my grandfather was in the hospital bed, telling the doctors not to revive him. He did not want to be on life support at all. He was prepared to be with God in heaven. It has been so many years, and I still think about them. I even shed tears at times. What keeps me going is knowing that the legacy must continue and that I have to live out what my grandfather taught me. I also have this mindset to please my parents and, of course, God. After all the sacrifices they have made for me, I do my best to make good decisions and represent them in a positive light.

As I get older, I understand that the only person you should want to or strive to be better for is yourself. One of my greatest struggles was caring more about others' opinions of me instead of accepting my opinion about myself. I will definitely be vulnerable in this book and step out of my comfort zone. I believe freedom comes only when exposure takes place.

3

I'm Not Perfect (Insecurities)!

"So God created man in his own image, in the image of
God created he him; male and female created he them."

GENESIS 1:27

This scripture is the beginning of the creation of men
and women. It is the explanation of how we got here
as human beings. The fact that we have security in the
God that created us in His image, we must always be confi-
dent, right? We should always feel like we are enough because
God has created us in His own image. The truth is that even
with this knowledge, it can still be challenging to know that

13

you are perfect the way God created you. Especially as a young woman, I battled with my physical appearance. I battled with low self-esteem. The truth is I battled feeling like I wasn't enough, even though I have been saved and in a relationship with Jesus Christ since the age of thirteen. I have gone through situations that influenced my low-self esteem.

Have you ever thought about how others perceived you? I have. I hear all the time, "You shouldn't care about what people think about you" or "People's opinions about you don't matter." I agree that God's opinion is what is of supreme importance. However, the insecurities that I battle with are not ones I was born with or one's I choose to have, but insecurities that people have highlighted. What I mean by this is that I probably would have been fine in my social relationships if people did not point out my greatest insecurities. But, that's people for you. We have to come to an understanding that words hurt. We must ask ourselves the most important questions. Is it really true that opinions don't matter?

Let's consider that we live in the 21st century where image is so important, especially now that we live in this modern age where technology is vital. Many people try to maintain an image. This image is highly influenced by one social group in society. Social image is what you think about yourself and what you want people to think about you. This generation, generation z's, confidence is built on social media trends found on Facebook, Instagram, Tik Tok, Snapchat, and many other platforms that cause one to think less of themselves. Beauty is now determined by how many likes you get. This concept of keeping up your image is heavy in the church as well. Many people are stuck on supporting or attaching themselves to popular people in society rather than having true anointing from God. Even on the dating scene, people are so focused on how someone looks physically, and they don't have the same concerns about whether the person is kind, has a good heart, is a good listener, or all of the qualities that truly matter in a relationship, at least a long-term relationship.

Anyways, I just went on a tangent. I'll open up about my dating later. It is a lot to unfold. But, social media has had some positive effects on my life. I was not on social media until the age of thirteen. I had an Instagram at thirteen. My parents didn't allow me to get a Facebook page until I was sixteen years old. However, despite me being able to post pictures of myself, perceiving myself as happy, I honestly was not happy. I was being bullied in school. I was never able to fit into a clique. I only had one friend, Jade, who would try to comfort me when someone bullied me. I remember one time I was going to class, and this random person said something like, "Eww, what's that all over your face?" My heart broke with that statement. Most of the insults were about my acne and because I was in the same grade as my younger sister. That added a whole different level of insults that I had to endure. I have a sister who is eleven months younger than me. We were in the tenth grade together because I got left behind in sixth grade due to failing the math state exam. I had to deal with questions like, "Why are you not a junior yet?" and "Did you get left behind?" Obviously.

I had difficult experiences in middle school, junior high school, and high school. I guess you can say I was the odd ball out. When people would talk about my skin, I would cry because I would battle with it at home, and now I had to go out in public, and people had to mention something about my skin. I remember there were times at home when I would walk into the bathroom and turn off the lights because I did not want to see my face. It was really that bad. My sisters would ask me, "Why do you have the lights off?" My confidence and self-esteem were so low. I also would walk with my head down low because I didn't want people to see my face. I didn't want people to see me. I had enough strangers, family members, and even church people saying stuff about an insecurity I was aware of. People would say, "Oh, she would be so pretty if she didn't have all those things on her face," or just flat out ask, "What is that on your face?" I can't believe that people think that words don't hurt because I was dying inside.

I also was insulted at church by "God's people." One guy at church said, "Oh, you should go get some Black Soap from down the street for your face." How rude is that? *Don't you think I know I have skin problems?!* I had tried so many different medications for my face. I tried the whole Proactive kit when it was first popular, and there were so many commercials saying this is the best acne medication to use. I used it for a while, and it worked for a little while, but it was expensive, and I couldn't keep using it. And let me say that it was not the miracle skin care kit that commercials made it to be. I didn't have a job, so my parents tried getting different medications to make me feel better. My dad even took me to his dermatologist to get advice. That's when I found something that helped, but it was also expensive. Thank God that I had insurance under my dad, though. Then my family moved, so I needed to change my dermatologist. It took some time to find a new dermatologist.

Let me tell you. The time I went without a dermatologist when I moved was stressful for me. I felt myself getting depressed. Eventually, I found one right around the corner from my church. I've been going to this dermatologist for almost two years now. This is the best medication I have used yet. However, I still have an issue with my skin. Even when I got a couple of pimples, I would get upset and worried that I would not look pretty anymore. Once I was very suicidal over my skin. My dermatologist would say, "Bacteria or dirt does not cause acne; oil does." However, at times, I feel like I look dirty. The truth is that I needed to heal and be freed from the opinions of others. I needed to love myself and my flaws. One day I asked my mother, with tears in my eyes, over a text, "When do you think I will stop dealing with low-self esteem?" She said, "You already are. You are a thousand times better than you were last year." I said, "Yeah, I mean, sometimes my skin still bothers me even though I use medication."

She replied, "You have to remember that no one is perfect. Everyone and I mean EVERYONE is dealing with something that they wish they could change. But there has to come a time where you just have to accept the things you can't change. Remember, your face is something that bothers you, and most if not everyone can't even see what you see wrong." I appreciatively replied, "Yeah, you're right."

Although I haven't been insulted about my skin in years, the past creeps up on me. You know? I still think about what people said. At times, the insults that I received about this specific insecurity still plague me. I appreciated the much-needed conversation I had with my mother because I would go to sleep and think about my skin, constantly questioning myself. *Why do I look the way I look? Why can't I be someone else? Why can't I look like other young women?* I was comparing myself to other women. I was fortunate to find Cheryl Martin's book, *Distinctly You: Trading Comparison & Competition for Freedom & Fulfillment,* which thoroughly expresses why comparing oneself is not productive, and how it actually bruises one's self-esteem, causing us to feel less of ourselves. Cheryl Martin states, "We can accomplish God's purposes in our own packaging when we make the most of what we have" (Martin, 2016).

This quote is very encouraging because, as my mother said, "Everyone has something they would like to change about themselves." But it's up to us to change what we can and accept what we can't change.

That's so true. Whatever the insecurity you have, it is extremely important not to compare. I agree with her. We should do our best to change as much as we can about a flaw or try to better something that we find unattractive about ourselves. Then it is our choice to accept what we cannot change. Of course, that's easier said than done. Also, even beyond that, words and actions both hurt. I would say words hurt deeper. Because if those words didn't hurt or bother me, I wouldn't remember or care today. But those words did hurt me. It takes work to get the thoughts out of your mind or forget the words people have said that have hurt you. I don't think all people who have said something about my skin meant harm. Some could have just been giving me the advice to make it better. But I didn't take it that way. I took some people's genuine help as insults. That is because I was guarded. That is because I was already hurt by people who insulted me because of my deepest insecurities. So I thought everyone was out to hurt me.

In my opinion, the best thing someone could have done was nothing. The best thing someone could have said was nothing. I still don't think anyone should highlight another person's insecurities that they have to accept already. We never know how hurt someone is about a flaw they have or an insecurity that someone is already struggling with. Even though it took some time for me to get over people's comments about my skin issues, I eventually got over the past. I learned that continuously reflecting on past issues and past hurt is not healthy. It is not healthy to ponder on the negatives in life. It is not healthy to focus on the wrong people have done to you.

I believe this because the good usually outweighs the bad. At every point of my life, the good outweighed the bad. I may not have been popular in school. I may not have been the image of beauty in school. But, I had a home with a family who loved me. I also had God. But, at the time, I did not feel Him there with me. I had a two-parent home with parents who loved each other. I never starved. I had many blessings. But, sometimes, it's much easier to focus on what is going wrong than what is going right. I had to practice this daily. I had to learn to compliment myself. By practicing loving myself more, I had to learn to stop replaying the negative words people have said about me and to me. I also complimented myself based on who I was as a person, not based on my physical. I constantly reminded myself how giving, kind, loving, sincere, intelligent, and helpful I was. I always reminded myself that I was an asset, that my life mattered. And in every moment that I began to feel less than a person and low self-esteem started to creep back in, God was always there to comfort me through prayers and reading His Word. He let me know that it is not the physical that makes me beautiful. It is my heart for Him. It is the light of Christ that shines through me. I found my worth through Christ's love.

Finding my worth through my relationship with Christ has given me the strength to do all of the public things I do for Christ. I would have never thought I would be able to go on social media to share the gospel with many people watching me. I would have never been able to lead a Christian club on a college campus without finding my worth in Christ. I would have still been stuck in the bondage of valuing people's opinions of me rather than focusing on God's opinion of me. When no one else was there to encourage me, God was always there to comfort me. God is always there with you in your darkest moments. I forgive those people who hurt me with their words unknowingly and knowingly. Forgiveness is what allows us to move on. Finding my worth in Christ made a huge difference in my life.

4

A False Escape (Defense Mechanism)

"For there is nothing hidden that will not be
disclosed, and nothing concealed that will not
be known or brought out into the open."

LUKE 8:17

I have to admit that some of the things I will talk about
in this chapter are things I had to pray on. I had to
pray on it to see if God really wanted me to share. But,
I must to free myself and others. Although I am a Christian, I
have to admit that I have not been perfect. I have fallen. I have

23

disappointed myself and disappointed God. My low self-esteem opened me to many traps. Although in grade school, my main insecurity was my acne, I was also going through issues with my hair. I hated that my hair was so short. I would always have my hair in box braids and weaves to cover my natural hair. Too much of the weave and braiding pulling my natural hair caused my hair to be damaged. For many years I wore box braids until one day, I went to take out the braids, and my hair was literally falling out in patches. I didn't know if I kept them in too long or if I was not taking care of the braids enough. But my hair was falling out, and I had patches on my head. I was devastated. My mom tried to help me fix what hair I had left, but the patches were difficult to cover up.

After this ordeal, I went natural—no more weaves or braiding. I was going to the dermatologist, so I asked about the patches. She took a magnifying glass and looked at my scalp. She said, "There's hair growing there. It could be iron deficiency because you are younger and still are getting a menstrual cycle. However, it can also be the braiding because it pulls the hair." I ended up getting recommended to a hematologist, a physician specializing in researching, diagnosing, treating, and preventing blood disorders and disorders of the lymphatic system. When I went, they took blood. At first, my doctor thought it could be the autoimmune disease called Alopecia Areata. My mom thought it was stress because I was stressed about my skin, getting back into school, and trying to find a job at the time. So, stress made it worse. When my test result came back, it was negative for alopecia and any other illnesses. However, I did lack a little iron. The doctor prescribed hair medication that I used for a while, but I found a natural hair oil, and it worked miracles. All the patches grew back. Then I went to get my hair cut to a short hair cut to even out. I have maintained hair growth by not pulling it or putting too much pressure on it. Since I am natural now, I use coconut oil which helps my hair grow so much. I love the haircut. I have kept my hair cut for almost a year now.

The fact that I was hiding behind the weave and covering up my insecurity did not help me but hurt me. If you do not deal with the issue, you can not heal from the issue. If you do not expose what causes you pain, it will not disappear; it will fester. It took me a long time to understand that. My insecurities even created a defense mechanism within me and caused me to overcompensate in other areas of my life. *Simply Psychology* (Saul Mcleod) defines defense mechanisms as "psychological strategies that are unconsciously used to protect a person from anxiety arising from unacceptable thoughts or feelings" (McLeod, 2019). There are many different defense mechanisms, such as denial, repression, projection, displacement, rationalization, and so many others. My defense mechanism was compensation. I still compensate to this day, even though I am working on it. That's the beauty of life, though. Being honest with yourself and others is honorable. Knowing that there are things I still have to work on keeps me humbled. Psych Central expresses compensation as "A process of psychologically counterbalancing perceived weaknesses by emphasizing strength in other arenas" (Grohol, 2022).

I have always maintained good grades as a student from middle school to now college. So, I compensated by doing good in school and being a good child at home. I felt that being on the honor roll, maintaining A's & B's, and being on the dean's list defined who I was. Therefore, I was devastated when I did not get honor roll or recognition. As a psychology student, I understand the mind is a powerful tool that can be used positively or negatively. It could even mask something negative as positive and something positive as negative. Although it's good that I wanted to always be on the honor roll, it was negative for me to allow that to define who I was. Nothing on this earth should define our happiness because things can change, and things can be taken away.

It's so important to find happiness within yourself. The truth is that our hearts and mind are interconnected within us. According to *Everyday Health,* "A sudden emotionally or physically stressful event could trigger a condition known as stress cardiomyopathy or broken heart syndrome" (Etienne, Rapaport, McPherson, Derrow, 2020). (When I found this information, I thought it was both relatable and truly explains why many people like myself have looked for ways to protect themselves and compensate for what we lack. Ever since I was dealing with being bullied because of my skin, I developed low self-esteem. The low self-esteem caused me to want to over compensate because I felt like I was not enough. Webster's dictionary defines overcompensation as "an excessive reaction to feeling of inferiority, guilt, or inadequacy leading to an exaggerated attempt to overcome the feeling" (Merriam-Webster. com, 2022). I felt inferior throughout grade school, and it was expressed through my need to receive success in education. Because of this, my social life was non-existent. To be fair, I was an old soul. I liked old school music. I'm a fan of 70s and 80s hits like "Heaven Must Be Missing An Angel" by Tavares or "Midnight Train to Georgia" by Gladys Knight and the Pips. I was not like every other teen in my life. I was always different. I always had a mature mindset.

I had one close friend named Jade in the 9th, 10th, and beginning of the 11th grade. She was my best friend until I moved to the suburbs from the city. Before and after that period, I had not had a close friendship. I was more of the quiet and shy type of person. People would describe me as a total teacher's pet. I was mainly focused on getting good grades. I was the last chosen to be on a team in gym class—every single time. I was someone's last choice. I never felt like enough for anyone. This affected me negatively because I developed a defense mechanism. I built a complete wall between me and any person that tried to be friends with me or anyone who tried to get to know me. I was trying to protect myself from any further pain that I could possibly go through. Even though these people that tried to get to know me were not the ones to hurt me. I still took out my pain on them.

Consequently, I felt so lonely, even though I had six younger sisters and an older brother in my corner. I could not see that they were for me because I was blinded by the pain that strangers inflicted. Even with my sisters, I judged them because of the friends they chose to be around, not knowing that I was still hurt deep within myself because I was not enough for people my age. I did feel excluded amongst my siblings at times. They had friends and people who were interested in them. There's a saying that "misery loves company." I'm not sure that is always true. People battling issues often need someone to have compassion and be empathetic toward them. Because I couldn't fit in, I was miserable. I expected my sisters to identify with what I was going through. The truth is they could never understand because one cannot really understand the effects of something they have not experienced. Also, they're my younger sisters. I'm supposed to be the person they go to about social issues, right? Honestly, I guess I was a little jealous that they had a flourishing social life. While desiring friends, I was still very standoffish and had a mindset that if anyone wanted to be friends, they had to approach me and pursue me. How counterproductive is that? I know. A friendship should be a reciprocation of care from both parties. Both people should be giving and taking. If there's no reciprocation, the relationship is least likely to last.

In addition to overcompensating, I was introduced to pornography. I hate to admit that I indulged in pornography because I am a Christian, and I was a Christian when I was introduced to it. I was young and going through self-esteem issues, and the enemy came in. I remember because I was still in grade school. That's when I look back, and I remember bits and pieces of how it started. I understand the simple truth that satan places tricks and roadblocks in your life to distract you, to trap you. I was unaware of this at the time. How did it start? I was exposed to pornography as a defenseless and sheltered young pre-teen. As a pre-teen, I was not exposed to a lot.

My parents sheltered my siblings and me. They kept us in the church. I am grateful for this. They taught us about God and everything. They sheltered us. However, at the time, I was unaware of satan's devices. I don't blame my parents because they were young when they married and had children. My mother was nineteen years old, and my dad was twenty-one when they married. Despite being so young, they were great parents. They supported all eight of their children. They provided stability, food, clothes, a home, and extras like electronics and toys that we begged for. They had nothing to do with my secret bad habit. I did not go looking for this, but somehow it found me. Since I was experiencing bullying and loneliness, I believe it put me in a place of vulnerability. I was just walking around a family member's house playing and doing child activities when I came across a laptop that I didn't know then but found out was pornography. At that time, I would also come across what I now know were sex toys. My parents did not know because I did not tell them. I really don't want to shame them by saying this. I was introduced to it when they did not know. I was actually caught once. I fell asleep on my phone and when I woke up my phone was gone. Of course, I was called into my

29

parents' room about what they had seen. I was so scared. They asked angrily, "Where did you get this from?" I said, "I got it from Kevin." Kevin is my older brother. He didn't live with us, so I thought it would be easy to blame him even though I found it on a laptop at my family member's house. Who knows whose laptop it was. I didn't. Today, I realize whose laptop it was and whose toys they were. But I forgive her.

After they found that on my phone, I did get punished by getting my phone taken away, but that didn't stop it. I just became sneakier about it. It was a secret problem. I feel so bad about it now because I realize that it is completely against God. Many people try to justify pornography use because it is so popular. But, it is wrong. Just because something is popular doesn't make it right. As a believer, I am especially supposed to set the standard and only do what is right in God's eyes. However, I do admit that I fell short. But then I felt empty, alone, and I did not like myself. Like any other addiction, it is easy to start but hard to stop. I dealt with this for some time. I would stop watching the videos, and then at one point, I was reading erotic literature. This is no better than the first. I was convicted. Eventually, I turned to God for deliverance from it, and He helped me because how it was introduced was not my fault. However, making the change is totally my responsibility. Many people have been introduced to pornography and have addictions to it. Many people also have addictions to alcohol, partying, having sex, lying, manipulating, cheating, and even drugs to try and fill an empty void within them. It all comes from hurt, in my opinion.

Even in the church, some people battle with it. But, sex is rarely talked about in the church. I believe this is the problem in why there are so many young ministers having babies out of wedlock. It is important to be educated on sex, teaching the dangers of diseases and soul ties. It is even important to talk about how having a child will change one's life—talking about hormones is also very important. If most people were honest, they would say that their flesh made them do some negative things. The hormones start rising at the early pre-teen stage. Although I understand the feeling of urgency will rise, it is important not to give into the flesh. Matthew 26:41 says, "Watch and pray, that ye enter not into temptation: the spirit indeed is willing, but the flesh is weak." We are constantly fighting against what our flesh wants daily. We have the commandments, and the Word of God tells us the standard of how we should conduct ourselves. But, that doesn't mean the flesh will not fight against the spirit.

Having self-control is the biggest thing in this battle of flesh against the spirit. The first step is calling sin as sin and wrong as wrong, not trying to justify it. Acknowledging that you need help from God is the first step. In my experience, I learned the power of self-control and prayer. Knowing my story and my process of getting free can help anyone get free from any bad habit. I know that God can free anyone from any addiction.

5

Free Yourself

"So if the son sets you free, you will be free indeed."

JOHN 8:36, NIV

I didn't want to do it anymore because I felt wrong doing it. I felt convicted every time I would read or watch something. Although there's pain in me talking about my battle with this, it is very important for me to highlight that addictions happen in the church. One thing about being in sin is that it may be enjoyable at the moment. Then when the enjoyment is over, you're left there to think about the sin you have committed. But I couldn't stop because I was still dealing

33

with the bullying, low self-esteem, and the lack of self-worth. I was so lost. Everything that was said to me by people in the church, at school, or at home by my siblings just made me go deeper into it. I was not walking in forgiveness, but I was carrying hurt within me because I was not normal and couldn't fit in. I can admit that my attitude was pretty bad in school because of what I experienced. And because I did walk around upset, I was so hated in school because my attitude was so bad due to the bullying. I can admit that. But, I don't believe anything that happened to me in school should have happened. It wasn't like I was going to people asking for issues. I would stay in my own lane. I got into two physical fights in school. One was with this boy named Craig. Yes, I fought a boy in school. I kept complaining to my parents that he was bothering me. I would walk into class, and he would just frown at me. I even wrote a journal entry before the fight happened.

December 1, 2015: Journal

I am feeling a little disappointed today, mainly because of my social issues. A boy has a problem with me, and I never did anything to him. He says things under his breath and rolls his eyes at me. So today, I decided to move away from him because I do not want to deal with immature behavior. I feel that I know God has a plan for me because I feel like maybe he is trying to get me alone, and whatever he is doing is really working because

I only have four or five so-called 'friends.' Oh, never mind, I only depend on God, but I have four of five people I talk to a lot. The rest of them just speak to me when they feel like it. I notice the relationship between all of the 'friends' is they care about each other very much. First, I thought maybe it was just because I didn't speak to anyone. But I was wrong about that because I always speak and am nice. It is just so difficult to receive what I give to people. Through this experience, I am learning that people won't treat you as well as you treat them, and it is never a problem to be alone. Even after all of this, I have nothing to complain about because there are people dying. I just pray that God blesses me to be able to socialize better and get rid of whatever bad things people see that make them want to have an issue with me.

Soon after this journal entry Craig and I were out in the school hallways fighting. He was suspended after the fight because I complained about him so many times. They waited until a fight happened to do something about this boy. I can't believe it. The second and last physical fight I had in high school was when two people jumped me. Again, here I was complaining about another student named Calvin, who kept bothering me in class. All the vice principal and other faculty members said was, "We can't do anything because it hasn't been physical." So I had to go to class every day feeling unsafe and worried about what would happen. One day I was walking in the hallway to the bathroom from class, and my hair was tugged from behind by a girl. I didn't recall having any issues with a girl. This guy Calvin didn't want to fight me himself, so he got a girl to sneak attack me. She pulled my hair from behind. It happened so fast. Once it was over, they both just walked away from the scene.

I cried profusely when I got up, seeing my hair on the floor. I was so embarrassed because people were looking outside the hallway from classrooms like it was a show. Nobody helped me. I was so broken by this. No one was there for me when I went through this unexpected attack. I walked and ran into security. The security guard took me to the main office, where I called my mom because my dad was at work. My mother, myself, and the girl were sitting in the school's office talking about the issue. This girl was basically a convict. She stayed in trouble. She had a bad record. This was her last straw, being suspended. She was suspended, but I wasn't because I didn't do anything. I remember just looking in the mirror at home just seeing all the hair that I had lost. I had literal patches of bald spots on my head. It was an unexpected attack I had no time to fight back. I was thrown to the floor, and then the two people ran away.

I felt helpless that day. I felt like I should've done more to protect myself. I felt weak. I looked at myself as a weak person. This fight, or really the attack, did more than take my hair. At that moment, my trust in people was taken away. I'm not so trusting anymore. It takes a lot for someone to get close to me because of this incident. I admit my mouth was reckless sometimes, and my attitude was bad, but I never verbally attacked people who didn't try to bully me. Bullies get upset when the victim does not want to be a victim anymore and chooses to retaliate.

In both circumstances, I questioned, "Where was God?" I claimed God so heavily in my life, but I was in trouble and couldn't find Him around. Therefore, not only was I retaliating against people but also retaliating against God by watching pornography. Trauma in one's life can cause addiction. It can create a monster within someone. Being hurt by someone or something can cause significant issues. On top of the low self-esteem, I developed major trust issues. Looking at the different intervention shows, most people going through drug addiction, alcohol addiction, bulimia, and anorexia have had some traumatic experiences happen. Even criminals in jail have experienced traumatic things like rape, abandonment from family, feeling alone, childhood abuse, and neglect. So many other traumatic issues can cause bad habits to form. Although I'm glad I didn't turn to worse things like drug abuse, crime, etc. I talk about pornography openly because I want those who have dealt with it or are dealing with it to know that they can be free through Christ. What I had been through didn't cause me to start, but it made me vulnerable enough to accept when presented. The logic or the reasoning behind it may seem strange. Some people might not understand it. But, it was a distraction, not knowing that I was really affecting myself. Every time I tried to stop, I would relapse like a true addict. I finally told someone I knew closely that I indulged in watching pornography. We were riding in the car from a fast-food restaurant, heading to get my mom's birthday gift. I said, " I have something to tell you." She asked inquisitively, "What do you have to tell me?"

I say worriedly, "I don't want you to look at me differently." I actually started crying because I was very ashamed. She was getting nervous. Finally, fifteen minutes later, I shared the secret. She said, "Oh, that's it. I would be worried if you didn't because you are going through that stage." Once I shared it, I did feel better since I finally told someone. We had a joke from that moment on because I seemed always to break down when driving back home from this fast food place. Although the statement made me feel better, I knew that I could not continue to watch this. This is a sexual sin. So I decided to stop for myself, with the help of God, of course. I felt wrong. Also, I wanted to honor God and feel closer. I know that we won't be perfect, but we must examine ourselves and change the activities that don't please God.

"Examine yourselves to see whether you are in the faith; test yourselves" (2 Corinthians 13:5, NIV). Do you not realize that Christ Jesus is in you — unless, of course, you fail the test? The truth is someone won't change if they don't want to change. They won't change if they feel like change isn't needed. I wanted to change, so I took steps to change. It did not happen overnight, but I never gave up. First, I deleted Google. Porn is so accessible, so I made it inaccessible. One can quickly go on the Internet and find it so this deleting the internet was a significant step in the right direction for me. Secondly, I picked up my writing again. I wrote more to keep myself busy and focused.

When I indulged in this sin, I was functioning, but I was still bound. That's what I ran to for temporary comfort. I put my true passion, which is writing, to the side. Writing my feelings down on paper has really helped with my next step: forgiving those who hurt me and forgiving myself for allowing them. There may be a craft that you had put down or stopped due to being distracted. I encourage you to pick that back up. Get that passion back for what you once loved to do, which is positive and good for your growth. Proverbs 16:27 says, "Idle hands are a devil's workshop; idle lips are his mouthpiece." To me, this speaks to having too much idle time. If we are not working or doing, we can easily get caught up in bad behavior. It can be easy to get caught in sin when doing nothing. Always have a passion for something. Use the gift that God has given you.

Lastly, my most important step is fasting and praying—something I always have found an essential part of the Christian walk. "Watch and pray so that you will not fall into temptation. The spirit is willing, but the flesh is weak" (Matthew 26:41 NIV).

If I don't spend at least three hours praying and worshiping God, I feel my spirit become weak. Of course, I pray every day, but I always need one day in the week where I spend hours of undivided attention to God. As I take my relationship with God more seriously, I become stronger mentally, emotionally, physically, and spiritually. I'm not talking about no ten-minute prayer. I spent four to five hours crying out to God. I repented, and He forgave. I knew He heard my cries because I felt His positive energy and presence. I would play instrumental worship or just soft gospel music and pray.

God would just move heavily, and I would begin to cry. I'm so thankful for the quality time with God because it is not conditional. I can feel his love for me. It is tangible. I appreciate the fact that I can talk to God about all of my past and current insecurities, failures, and issues. Throughout all of this, I am thankful that I overcame this sin and that I did not allow it to overcome me. I have learned that since God gives grace to us constantly, we as believers should find a place within us where we have grace for ourselves and others, even those who have hurt us. I went through so much shame and guilt for dealing with this at this time. Now that I'm free from it because of my relationship with Christ, I am so much happier.

However, we must expose to become free from what is holding us down. Many people have dealt with this same issue and are looking for help to get free from it. This not only speaks to what I dealt with, but sex, in general, is a huge issue in society. If you're battling with fornication (sex outside of marriage), adultery (cheating on a spouse), or pornography, you can be delivered through prayer. Because I was freed from my bad habit, with the help of God, I know that anyone else can be free and live free. When I was battling hurt and pain, I didn't feel God with me. God healed me from the hurt so that I could be free. If you're still carrying hurt, God can heal it. If you want to be free from habits that grew from hurt, God can break those habits. Nothing is too hard for him. Honestly, God healing me from the hurt and freeing me has been a reminder for me. It has been a reminder to continue to lift a standard for Christ and promote a holy lifestyle no matter what I'm going through. The deliverance I experienced from this bad habit has strengthened my love and boldness for Christ. Everything I do for Christ, I do with boldness because He did the work that I couldn't do within myself. He reached down into the deep places that I felt I couldn't tell anyone about because of the shame and guilt. This is why I'm so committed to Him. This is why I'm so committed to making His name great on the earth. This is why I push for a relationship with God so consistently because He saved me from me.

What Hindered You?
Poem by Tatyana Ferrer

When I would do good, evil was always present.
All have sinned and fallen short of God's
glory, at least that's what they say.
I ask God to forgive me when I pray.
Forgive me for the sins I committed
knowingly and those unknowingly.
You may ask yourself, why do I keep smoking,
drinking, fornicating, or lying.
Many of the things I know are wrong.
Hanging around people in places
where I know I don't belong.
What about those secret things? Or does it
not bother me because no one knows?
So, I think no one knows. But God knows all.
Everything is naked before the eyes of God.
He catches me when I fall.
I am so grateful that even though He knows my wrongs,
He gives me chance after chance to get back in the race.
I guess that's why God says we are saved by His grace.
Thank God I don't have to depend on my own righteousness.
Thank God that Jesus Christ took all of
our sins upon Himself at Calvary.
Now we all have the chance to live right in the eyes of God.

Knowing that when we confess our sins to
Him, He is faithful to forgive us.
On earth, we will never be completely perfect.
Like my grandfather would say, although
our souls get saved, our flesh doesn't.
I have learned that we have to give ourselves
grace when we disappoint ourselves.
God, as our Father, is patient with us.
Shouldn't we follow the God we passionately trust?
Don't allow the guilt, regret, and shame cause
you to stop growing, developing, and becoming
all that God has called you to be.
Open your eyes and see that every day
is an opportunity to recommit.
Recommit to your walk with God because,
despite all we do, His love remains true.

6

God's Design

"Therefore shall a man leave his father and his
mother, and shall cleave unto his wife: and they
shall be one flesh. And they were both naked, the
man and his wife, and were not ashamed."

GENESIS 2:24-25, KJV

I think it is important to talk about sex, whether single
or married. We should be able to talk about God's
design and the risks. Although I struggled in the past,
my opinions about sex remain the same. I have never had sex.
I never will until married. Sex is to be an act only done in

45

marriage. At sixteen, I had a ceremony devoted to saving sex for marriage. That was my sweet 16. I have kept that vow. So, it is still possible to wait for God for sex and hold on to your virginity or be celibate. Sex is an act meant to happen between a husband and his wife, which means between a biological woman and a biological man. It is important to realize that many things in society have become popular due to people experiencing difficult things in life, like being molested, raped, and used sexually for years. Some have experienced so much sexual trauma in their lives that they believe having sex outside of marriage is right. Some people are not aware of God's design for sex. This is why I believe it is so important to hear people's stories and teach them the right way. I believe as Christians, we should acknowledge the pain and encourage the right way. It is necessary to clarify this because since technology has evolved, the world has changed and, laws have been passed, many people have created and adopted ways to make sexual sin right. People have now created different pronouns such as they/them, he/him for people who look like women, and she/her for people that look like men. Unfortunately, those in charge push the idea that people can create their own genders in society. They can live according to what gender they feel like rather than who God made them. This all comes from not knowing identity in Christ. This comes from not knowing my Christ loves us in our sin. It is important to know that Christ loves you even when we have sinned. Once we understand the true love that Christ has for us, we don't have to walk in shame or guilt. But, we can walk in confidence, knowing that God has forgiven us. When we begin to understand that Christ has forgiven us, we can walk in truth. Walking in truth requires us to know his design. God's design is not man's design. God created man and woman. A man has a penis, and a woman has a vagina. These are the parts that identify male or female. So many people have said they felt like they were a woman even though they were born in a male's body. Unfortunately, the environment impacts people's thought processes and sexuality. A child does not come out born knowing what being gay is or what pronouns are. He or she has an identity that is easily male or female, not they. There are actually adults who put this confusion on the children. Saying, "Oh, why can't a boy child play with dolls?" Like, is that a serious question? It's ridiculous.

This I was born gay, and not a choice concept kills me. God created two genders successfully and with no mistakes. And I don't dislike gay people. However, I just don't believe I should change my views about how it affects children. This gay agenda is taught. In this world, the youth are being bombarded with this gay agenda. We see it on TV, in schools, and even in certain music. I remember working at a fast-food restaurant, and it was "pride" month. They hung up a rainbow flag poster in the restaurant. That disturbed me. But it's public property, so it wasn't my business. However, they then wanted people to wear rainbow masks and shirts with rainbows. I chose not to participate because I don't support that lifestyle. There were gay people there, and I would speak to them and be nice. I always believe as Christians, we should always show love. But, participating is different from loving someone going through it. I support freedom from the lifestyle.

We have to be so bold in our love for Christ that we don't care about the opinions of the world, we value honoring the Word of God, and we value what God says about sex. This is all knowledge from God's Word. He did not make any mistakes when He designed us. This is a part of why people are bound by sexual sin. They don't understand the plan of God. If the law says it's okay, but God says it's not, most people go with what is culturally acceptable. As Christians, as followers of Christ, we must desire to please God with our bodies. This takes denying our flesh daily. I know this isn't easy because I have struggled. But, I recognize the importance of being an example. Of course, as Christians, we won't be perfect because we are human. However, each day we have to fight our flesh and be the example for people who don't Christ. I know that people choose a lifestyle because of the trauma in their childhood or how they were raised. I understand that our hormones are really strong, especially as young adults; they tend to rise. How we overcome fleshly desires is by crucifying our flesh daily. We must walk in the spirit. We must strengthen our spirit through prayer, worship, connecting with other believers, and reading the word of God. No matter how technology advances, God's way is the best. No matter how hard it is to overcome sin, it is possible with Christ. Since the beginning of creation, He ordained for sex to be an act done only in the sanctity of marriage between a man and woman. Many people today believe that this thought is an old-fashioned or, as they would say, a played-out thought process. Even though the Bible says a man and his wife became one flesh, they'll try to misconstrue scripture by picking parts of it to rationalize the lifestyle of sin they choose to live. Sadly, fornication, homosexuality, adultery, pornography, and promiscuity are common. Not only in the world we live in but also in the church. Yes, I said it. Many people in the church go to church wearing a mask to cover up the sin in their lives. Although we fall short, it's a part of our human nature to do so. God still has caused us to fight to live righteous lives.

Hebrews 10:26 says, "For if we go on sinning deliberately after receiving the knowledge of the truth, there no longer remains a sacrifice for sins." God knows that we will fall short. But, some people don't want to be free from sin. There are people who don't view their sin as sin. They don't try to change what is displeasing to God. They really please their flesh. The truth is that when God sees you trying to do something different, He honors that when you attempt to obey Him and live without sin. But, as the scripture says, if you continue in something you know is wrong, there is no more sacrifice for your sin because you have rejected God's help. But, the beauty of God is that when you come to Him broken and battling with bad habits, He'll deliver you because He sees your desire to live right. Living right is for us to be closer to Him. Living a sinless life isn't always easy. It takes spiritual strength. It takes faith.

There's some message that has kept so many people down: the "eternal security" message. This is the message that preachers preach that once you receive Christ, you will automatically go to heaven regardless of how you live your life before you die. This message says that there's no hell. That God doesn't expect anything from us as believers. It's like saying a student who goes to class but never does his homework will pass simply because he goes to class every day. The answer is that eternal security traps people into deeper bondage. It has people thinking that what is a problem is not a problem. God doesn't expect perfection. He knows that we will sin. Jesus Christ died for our sins. But, He expects obedience and a life of holiness. The truth is that hell and heaven are both real. What determines our actions and how we live our lives determines where we go. Receiving Christ is the first step to a long journey of learning and growing through Christ. He requires obedience to Him.

Some people are good at hiding their sins. Others are so bad at hiding it or simply don't care to hide it. I see so many feminine male pastors, choir directors, and praise and worship leaders. Why is that? What about promiscuity? That's something I really don't hear talked about much. When you claim to be a woman or man of God, you are supposed to present yourself as such. There is a standard that every believer is called to live up to. This is not just physical. But, this is based on lifestyle; how you present yourself to the public matters, for both men and women. I believe self-worth and provocative clothing has a relationship. I don't believe having standards in how we dress is wrong or being old. It's a reflection of self-respect and self-worth. When you know your value, you don't sell yourself short. I always live by the thought that covering up makes you interesting. It makes someone say, *wow, she's a mystery.* Many women feel the need to wear provocative clothing or clothing that shows a lot of skin to attract guys. But that actually attracts the wrong attention. It attracts someone who wants your body and not to get to know you. A respectable guy would love that you don't display your body to everyone. The one sent by God will love that you respect yourself. "Therefore, I urge you, brothers and sisters, in view of God's mercy, to offer your bodies as a living sacrifice, holy and pleasing to God — this is your true and proper worship. Do not conform to the pattern of this world, but be transformed by the renewing of your mind. Then you will be able to test and approve what God's will is — his good, pleasing and perfect will" (Romans 12:1-2, NIV).

How we present our bodies matters. Also, how we behave matters. I got on the women today. Now I have to deal with the guys. I've never seen a more entitled species of men. A lot of men think they're supposed to "have" you, whether it's kissing or sex. First of all, he's blessed even to be speaking to you. The woman of God is a gift to a man. Therefore, he should not expect things that are supposed to be in marriage. I'm not saying kissing is for marriage. Some may even try to save kissing for marriage. My thing is, I don't think it's appropriate to be in a bed together, making out, and definitely not having sex. It is important that we not put ourselves in places to be tempted. Giving a man sex is literally giving him all of you. That is why he must prove his love through commitment and marriage. That's not what I say. But, it is straight from the God who created us. That is why short skirts, sagging pants, see-through clothing, tight pants, crop tops, and many other trends or patterns of this world should not be adopted by those who claim to be children of God because it tempts one to have lust in their heart.

As Christians, we are supposed to have a different mindset from those in the world. We are supposed to be an example. Be an example that people can look up to and be inspired by. We don't have to be perfect. However, we are the example of Christ that people look at. How we present ourselves is how people will see us. Although many people make having standards a negative thing, standards prevent us from falling into escapable sin and unnecessary heartbreaks. Following the Word of God benefits us by protecting us from heartbreak, diseases, death, pregnancy, soul ties, depression, anxiety, and transferring of evil spirits. These things can be avoided by being obedient to God and living a holy lifestyle. We often find ourselves in inevitable situations; however, there are many preventable situations in life. The sad thing is that teachers in schools don't promote abstinence. They promote using protection. Plastic doesn't protect much. Contraceptives constantly fail. Abstinence until marriage is the best way. There are many excuses people use for having premarital sex. Like couples who aren't married say, "We're going to get married anyways," "It's okay because we are committed to each other," "A marriage certificate is just a paper," or "It's just foreplay." I'm pretty sure that couples make many more excuses to rationalize fornication, but those are quite popular.

Now for singles. Singles have many excuses like "Everyone is doing it," "I need the experience," "I want to be prepared for marriage," "My hormones are making me do it," and so many more. When we make excuses for sin, we will continue to be bound by what's holding us down. As a single myself, I understand that hormones are extremely powerful. If we did not have a sex drive, our bodies would not be working fine. It is a sign of the body not functioning properly. Desiring sex is normal. However, as believers in Christ, we are supposed to delay sex until marriage. If he hasn't yet proposed or you're not walking down the aisle, if those marital vows haven't been exchanged, don't fall for it. Don't fall for the eventually I will marry you lie. We shouldn't normalize sex outside of marriage. Let's normalize having high standards and getting the ring first. I realize that is not everyone's story. But, it saves a lot of heartache and pain. It creates a stable environment for children.

I have learned a lot by seeing so many single mothers in the church, even in my family. It is not God's plan for women to have four different baby daddies or for men to have four different baby mommas. I'm not shading anyone. I'm just presenting God's design. That is not a healthy lifestyle for the children, mother, or father. Not following God's design for sex being for marriage between a man and his wife brings unnecessary stress.

It births dysfunctional families. It births broken homes. The plan of God was for a man and woman to marry and create children in a stable, loving home with a firm foundation. I have compassion for those children born outside of marriage. These children either lack a father or a mother in their lives. The truth is as human beings, we need both a mother and a father in our lives. A mother provides things that a father cannot provide. A father provides things a mother cannot provide. As a young woman raised by both a mother and father, I know the importance of having both in your life. There have been times when my mom wasn't home at the moment, and I was able to go to my dad and vice versa. Having a two-parent has major benefits. A father demonstrates to a young woman how a man should treat her. He demonstrates to a son how to be masculine, have confidence, have male leadership, and demonstrate a positive image of love from a man's point of view. On the other hand, a mother provides comfort, sensitivity, femininity for a daughter, and advice on women's issues (menstrual, pregnancy, and menopause). Case and point are that a woman and man are both needed in the home. God has created us biologically, male or female, for a purpose. His design for the family dynamic is not wrong and cannot be changed. As a single believer, continue to wait on God and don't settle because you're lonely or want what people view as a "relationship goal." I remember my first relationship. We both went too fast. We were just into the boyfriend-girlfriend stage; we started posting because we wanted to jump on this "relationship goals" status. We barely knew each other. Shortly after posting these cute pictures, we broke up because I found out that we had no chemistry, and I ultimately was not attracted to him. The thing that sucked is that he came all the way from Texas to New York to visit me for one week. The whole time was awkward. I kept asking people, "Will we eventually feel better around each other?" I told my uncle I needed more time to feel him out. We were a whole couple. I could tell the guy was sad and hugged and tried to kiss me. I knew this because he would wait a long time to go back inside his hotel when I dropped him off. I would just hug him and say good night. He was honestly a great guy. He paid for my gas, poured it into my tank, bought dinner when we went out, held doors open, and even took me to go-kart racing. I eventually felt pressured to kiss him. So, I eventually kissed him or whatever. I never thought that I would initiate the first kiss. But, it was normal because we were in a relationship. But, I then had to tell him when he went all the way back home that I wasn't feeling the connection. I was so wrong because I should have told him sooner that I didn't find him attractive. It was a crazy situation. I was disappointed in myself because I publicized it, and now I'm breaking up with him. He was a gentleman and a committed Christian. That was attractive to me. However, just because two people are Christians doesn't make them automatically compatible. I've learned through this situation that long-distance is not my thing, to be upfront about how I feel if I'm not physically attracted to the guy, and not try to "make it work." I didn't want to reject him because he was so nice and godly. But, I've learned that being honest about what you feel in the beginning is important, not trying to be nice to someone just because you don't want to make them feel bad about being rejected. My current thoughts about sharing someone on Facebook or any other social media platform is that I won't do it in the dating stage or engagement stage. I will only post my husband. I have to have those documents and a wedding ring. Once you get those documents, you're good. If I don't have the paperwork. it's not going to happen. I think in the beginning stages, a relationship is fragile, and the two should really be trying to get to know each other on a deep level, like understanding if your personalities can co-exist is important. I believe a lot of the issue was that it was a long-distance relationship. I have to be able to spend that quality time with someone to get to know that person and feel close. FaceTime and phone calls are not enough. It's good to know this now, though. I apologized to the guy, and we are distant friends. I have an opinion about exes being friends or just men and women being friends in general. However, there's always more learning to do in relationships, whether friendships, dating, or marriage.

7

Who Am I Attracting, Lord?

"To every thing, there is a season, and a time
to every purpose under the heaven."

ECCLESIASTES 3:1, KJV

As a 22-year-old, I have had my share of dating, talking, and situationships. In these stories that I will share in this chapter, I have learned a lot about men or boys and what to look for. I have also learned about myself and what my non-negotiables are. I won't do long distance unless God says so. I can't date someone

57

who has the full-time ministry mindset, has no motivation, no relationship with Christ, isn't committed to a leader, and many others. Today's dating scene is so much different from what it used to be. We have a lot of standards in dating that I am strongly against. Maybe it's more of a lack of standards. Or we have things that I have seen become okay. That's not okay.

Unfortunately, many people settle because they don't want to be single. They want that relationship goals image that we see on social media. I used to accept messages from guys on social media who were not on my level. I'm talking about not being on my level mentally and spiritually. My esteem was very low, and therefore, I accepted anything. Don't get me wrong. I had a type. He had to be Christian, active in the church, and pursue me. Now I see that a lot of guys who claim to be Christian are not. Some people have the title without the fruits. They put on a facade for other people. But they're really living double lives. I used to be so caught up in getting a boyfriend or falling in love with the one. My focus was so much on having someone that I ignored the signs. I didn't know that everything I needed could be found in me. And now, knowing my worth has pushed me to encourage self-care and independence as a woman, especially as a woman of God.

I am all about women's empowerment. I am all about falling in love with yourself before trying to connect with someone else. How can you fall in love with someone when you don't know or love yourself? When you don't love yourself, you settle. From my experiences as a teenager, I have learned not to deal with disrespect or put up with any crap from any man. My father has also played a role in my respect for myself because he has respected my mom since the day I was born. He married her before having sex. He worked, went to school, and operated a church as a pastor. He did anything he had to do to provide for his family. A lot of guys today do not have that drive or motivation. They think the woman should work or "we should go fifty-fifty." I have a problem with that. Don't get me wrong; I'm all about a woman being able to reciprocate. The man shouldn't have to do all the work in the relationship. However, I believe there are certain characteristics that a guy should have. I believe he should have a good work ethic, be motivated, have a job, be respectful, loyal, committed, and of course, love God. I say this because if he doesn't have these qualities before dating, he will not change when you get married. He's going to be the same guy you met. So, I say it's fine to notice something that I don't like and move on. It takes strength to do that. I don't believe that, as a woman, I should try to change a man. As women, we cannot change men. Also, men cannot change women. That person has to want to change.

I have had some experiences that have influenced me to focus on being independent as a young woman to continue to do my work on myself and make myself better. I believe in being mentally, emotionally, and financially stable before getting married. Why do I say this? I say this because when you have confidence in yourself and depend on yourself and God, of course, no one can take anything from you, whether it's a roof over your head, car, money, or anything else. When you have created a stable lifestyle for yourself, you hold the keys to your life. So, in this case, I believe independence is necessary. However, when you start dating and when you get married, it should be a collective effort. It should be each person giving their all to the relationship, not just one person doing all of the work. I also believe that in your single stage, you must be approachable. Even though I am very independent, I believe in being approachable. I know that I can never expect to find the one or even get married without being approachable. Although I am single, I always promote making myself available and approachable. But, there are rules to being approachable. Don't give hints to someone you know you don't like. I used to do that because I liked the attention. However, I didn't even like the guy.

Even though I know all of the important steps to take now as a single Christian, I have some stories about "Christian" guys that I have talked to. The truth about my love life is that I only had one boyfriend. I had my first boyfriend at 21 years old. I know. That's crazy. I just was not interested in the dating scene in high school. But, I was very naive when I first talked to guys. I didn't know that guys just say things to get your attention. The first guy I talked to was called "Bryan." I met him in a church setting. One of the girls in church connected me to him. Well, she gave me his Facebook. This guy was a praise and worship leader and a preacher. He was what my family would call my type. My type has usually been the guy who's a preacher, musically inclined, or sings. It used to be that. Now I'm all about character and maturity. This guy was well-known in the church. A lot of girls liked him in the organization that I was in at the time. One thing about church girls is that they are attracted to titles. They'll like you if you're a praise and worship leader, musician, pastor, or just a well-known preacher. I didn't have that church girl mindset. I liked him because I was just interested in him. Once we started talking, it was fun. At that time, we would see each other at church or just go out together when we could go out. The first date was a movie. My aunt and dad would pick him up to take us to where we wanted to go. Another time we went out was to a church barbecue in the park. This is where things went wrong and started to unfold. The whole time I wanted to take pictures. He didn't want to. We took a picture, and he was so against posting it. Then, I received a call from someone, and this boy asked, "Who is that?" I should've said mind your business. But, it was a girl named Monica who knew Christian and knew that he had a girlfriend. She asked, "Are you with Bryan?" I said, "Yes, I am." She said, "I don't know if he told you this, but he has a girlfriend." I was in shock. All this time, he's standing here next to me talking about, "Don't tell her I'm here." I was so upset. It was so awkward because I found out while he was standing right next to me. I didn't even know the girl who called. I didn't even know how she got my phone number. I found myself in the middle of a messed-up situation. I told him not to talk to me and that he was going to hell.

"How are you supposed to be a man of God, and you lied?" I was so mad. All he was saying was, "I didn't lie. I just didn't tell you." I was emotional about the situation because I was betrayed. We talked for like two months, but it was still a messed-up situation. After finding out everything that he lied about, his girlfriend called me, and we talked. I explained that he never mentioned her or anything. I thought he was single. I clarified that he pursued me. She was angry at him and thankful that I told her. Of course, I stopped talking to him. And for a while, seeing him at church conventions was weird, and his presence irritated my soul. Another situation happened at a convention where I heard that he talked to a girl from my church. We were seventeen; this girl was fourteen. The girl was really fast for her age. Fast, meaning she was really desperate for attention. It showed in how she carried herself. Once, he messaged me and told me. I was so confused because we didn't talk anymore. So, I was confused as to why he was telling me. I didn't care about him. I didn't want anything to do with him.

Bryan: *"I just wanted you to know, I don't find interest in Sarah. We are just friends and nothing other than that. She told me she was sixteen. I found out she lied and that she's only fourteen. That would be soooooooo inappropriate‼ But I don't need you to hold a grudge against me. Please forgive me."*

Me: *"Oh, okay, that's interesting. Try not to get yourself in any trouble, lol. Be positive and go from monument to movement, leave the things in the past or people in the past, and move toward the higher calling in Christ. It's God you have to worry about, not me."*

Bryan: *"I felt like you just tried to be sarcastic and are not taking me seriously."*

Me: *"I am not trying to be sarcastic, and if you don't like her, why are you telling me? What role do I play in this? I'm moving on, trying to be truly saved and exude the love of Christ, and I just don't have time for the childish games. I'm not trying to be sarcastic, just being honest and aware."*

Bryan: *"Well, honestly, I was told you were crying, and that hurt me. I don't mean to hurt you in any way. I just wanted to get that off my chest. I'm sorry, just please forgive me and let's be friends and move on."*

Me: *"Lol, that's really funny because I don't cry over people, so sorry whoever told you that lied, and I certainly would never cry over you because I respect myself too much."*

Bryan: *"Is this your way of trying to put me down ?"*

Me: *"Not at all. That's not what I am trying to do, especially as a Christian, but I'm just not going to be disrespected. Like Bishop White said, 'we can't take disrespect or be disrespectful and know our worth and values.'"*

Bryan: *"How am I being disrespectful to you? I'm here trying to make up for what I did, being apologetic."*

Me: *"That's good, thank you. Why don't you just let me go? What are we doing here? I forgive, and I love you as Christ loves us."*

Bryan: *"This has nothing to do with letting you go. I'm just not trying to leave US on bad terms. I love everyone, and I expect*

63

everyone to feel the same for me. I don't want people disliking me, even though it does happen. But I just don't want YOU upset at me."

Me: *"I'm not upset. I decided that we are forgiving each other and that we are on good terms."*

Bryan: *"Thank you, my sister in Christ. Love."*

Since this conversation, we didn't talk consistently again. Once someone shows you their true colors, believe them. Don't deal with cheaters, lies, and disrespect if someone is talking to you while dating someone else. That is disrespect. That's not respect. That shows that you are a side piece. Never settle for being the side piece. If he doesn't want to express his care publicly, don't allow him to get close to you. What I mean is that if he can't even acknowledge you or take a quick pic, that's a problem. I'm not saying that he needs to post you on social media because I am in the mindset that we can't post if we're not married. But, if he's trying to be sneaky with you and doesn't want anyone to know that he's talking to you, don't stand for it. See the signs and know that you have to move on. I was glad that I had this experience because it taught me to look at the signs, do my research, go in peace, don't settle for a side piece position, and know that I don't have to settle. It was easy for me to let him go because I knew my worth in Christ.

Unfortunately, I went through another situation where I felt like I was doing too much in the relationship and he was doing too little. This guy's name was Scott. The first red flag was he lived in North Carolina. I live in New York. That's over eight hours' distance. This situation was partly why I don't do long-distance relationships. So, this guy was a youth leader and praise and worship leader. He pursued me on Facebook. At first, I looked at the distance, and it was not a problem. He approached me on social media in a positive and respectful way. This was a good sign for me. He knew me because of my ministry on Facebook. I have a Facebook ministry where I talk about topics related to Christianity. I motivate people to continue to live for Christ. I will talk about my journey in my relationship with God and ministry later on. So, this is how the first conversation went.

Scott: *"Good evening Woman of God. I must say I thoroughly enjoyed your live the other day. You're absolutely beautiful and stunning, and I would definitely like to be one of your friends. I can see myself growing with you in my corner."*

Me: *"Good afternoon. Thank you and TGBTG. I am glad it was able to bless you. Yes, it's important to have like-minded people in your corner."* 🙏

Scott: *"My my my, you have to inform me when you're going live again, or when you do your podcast."*

Me: *"I go live every Thursday at 8 pm. My podcast is usually posted Wednesday. I'll share it on my page. Bless you."* 😊

Scott: *"I def can't wait."*

Me: *"Thank you for the support."*

Scott: *"You're absolutely welcome."*

65

So, the conversations started really friendly. He watched my ministry and wanted to get to know me as a friend. This was all cool, but that friendship thing didn't last long. Immediately we were sharing too much and getting too comfortable too quickly. We started going into wedding colors and whether it was going to a big or small wedding. Of course, we weren't talking about each other. But we shouldn't have been implying at all. I mean, it's important to talk about marriage, kids, career, and all of those things. I believe if you're a Christian and you're talking to someone, your goal should be marriage, and therefore, if you're not ready for marriage, don't get into the dating thing. It is really important to let a friendship build before getting your feelings involved. We went from a friendship to talking about permanent moves in weeks. We didn't know each other long enough. One of the things that I overlooked was that he was too much into himself. The conversation was so much about him and what he was doing. What he had going on. He would always say, "Do you need me, or do you want me?" I was like, "I don't need anyone." There were times when we would be talking about something, and he wouldn't respond until two days later. I don't know about you, but that seems off to me. I would post things like, "It's so important to have someone pray with and for you." Then, I would literally tag his name. He wouldn't like it or even comment on it. I would give him the benefit of the doubt and say maybe he's not on social media right now. But I'll look on his page and see that he posted five minutes ago. Also, my ministry means a lot to me. I would go on live and talk about God, just speaking a message, and he was never on there. But he could comment to everyone else and post. Fast forward to when I got tired of it. The crazy thing was that I was going through so much to receive confirmation that I needed to move on. I asked, "How do you know if it's love?" They were like, "If you have to ask, it's not love." The true confirmation was his actions. He had not texted me in a couple of days, and I sent a serious message to him.

Me: *"Hey. I received my confirmation through prophecy and how you've been acting. I loved our conversations and everything. However, the chemistry is just not there. It shouldn't be something that is forced, but just 100% authentic. I don't want to waste each other's time any longer, and especially do not want to hold up one another from who God has called us to be with. I just feel I am not being 100% open. It just doesn't feel natural between us. When I share my ministry events with you, when I share my excitement with you, you just don't seem to share that excitement and care, even in the communication issue. I understand you have work and other responsibilities. So do I, which I share with you frequently. However, I believe that if you're truly interested in someone, you pursue them desperately, regardless of the distance. You show 100% interest in the person you're dating. You're not pursuing me desperately. Even I shared how grateful I was that you motivated me and helped me when I was going through spiritual warfare on Facebook. Also, I tagged you in an attempt for people to know who I was talking to. You literally did not like or comment. And other things that I post, you don't comment on or rarely like. I literally had to tell you that I commented on your profile picture. No one in public knows that you care about me or that we're even together. I need someone who will support me in my ministry and not lead me on, who will pursue me, not me having to tell you or force you. Anyways, I hope we can maybe still be friends or associates. But, this is not going to work. I know I am worth too much. Whenever you see or respond to this, don't take it to heart. I just can't force a connection any longer. I pray that God blesses you with your wife one day. I'm just not it. God bless."* 🙏

PS. Tatyana Ferrer

Scott: *"I understand where you're coming from. I don't be on FB like that tho... I may not show it on FB, but I do tell you over the phone about everything, and I see the things you tag me in. I voice it over the phone. I'm not afraid to show that I care or love you ... as far as a post, I didn't see your post today til just now. You're right; we're both worth so much, and neither one of us should feel uncomfortable being with each other. Yeah, we can remain friends or associates if you want to. Have a great life, Tatyana. If you want to talk to me more about God and stuff, you can."*

I was lowkey pissed by his response. *Have a great life, Tatyana? Are you serious?* My response to the weird moves that guys make changed. In the first story, I was so hurt and actually cried. In this situation, I was glad to be done with him. After this, he continued to check up on me. Sometimes I would answer, and other times, I wouldn't. But, I moved from the situation in peace. I looked at the actions and saw that I was being treated less than I deserved and moved accordingly. Unfortunately, a lot of women and men will stay in a relationship with someone who's not good for them simply to have someone there. A lot of women want to be married, and if the guy is taking too long, they'll propose. I would never be found proposing to a man. I am the prize. I am his blessing from God. To me, when women do that, I see the disparity. If a man wants you, he'll pursue you. There's no reason for it to be the other way around. If his mindset is not on marriage in the future, don't get with him to begin. Proverbs 18:22, NIV, says, "He who finds a wife finds what is good and receives favor from the LORD." You are that gift from God. You should not be treated as less than a gift. If you are younger or older and just going through a situation where you have to question whether you're in love or if this is the right relationship, the fact is that it's not. You have to learn to look at people's actions and ignore the words at times. If someone is saying all the greatest things in the world, make sure the words match up. I am glad I experienced these situations because they were tests to see if I knew my worth and if I would settle. Nope. I deserve more, and you deserve more too. I learned that I couldn't do long-distance relationships. I need maturity, someone who is truly saved and in relationship with Christ and supportive of me, whether in school, work or ministry. I expect support. The crazy thing is that after this conversation, we stopped talking, and a couple of months later, he hit me up on Instagram on Thanksgiving day.

Scott: "😢 *I miss u.*"

Me: "*It's so good to hear from you. Happy holidays. I hope you enjoy your family and great food!* 😊 🍁 🦃 "

Scott: "*Really?*"

Me: "*Really what? What are you confused about?*"

Scott: "*That it's good to hear from me.*"

Me: "*Oh. Yeah. Of course. I hope you're enjoying your family.*"

Scott: "*Why'd you delete me off Facebook, and why did you leave me? I thought we were a good couple? Our conversations were good. We talked about life and biblical stuff. We prayed with and for each other, gave each other advice.*"

Me: "*You didn't know what you wanted, and you weren't grateful for what you had. So I found someone who is. You're too late. You should have had this same energy when we were talking. Everything happens for a reason. God bless.*"

Scott: "*I didn't mean to push a button. My bad for even bothering you, Tatyana. I'll leave you alone.*"

Sometimes when you reject people or things, they'll try to come back for another chance with anything, whether it's a person who's not good for you or a habit that's not good for you, they will try to come back. But, it's up to you to learn from the lesson that God has given you. I've learned how to reject people in my life for the wrong reasons. It's strange that not putting up with crap would have people view you as upset or bitter. Just because I don't want to deal with you doesn't mean I'm bitter. It means I know my worth and refuse to waste time. From this situation, long-distance left a bad taste in my mouth. It's not for me. Knowing your worth is essential in your healing process and moving on from negative relationships.

I have found myself attracted to guys who had not felt the same way about me. I was interested, but they were not. They did not deserve me. Hopefully, you can identify when someone's not the one. So, I talked about having a fear of rejecting guys and dealing with someone sneaky, and now I'll talk about the too much guy. The too much guy is basically the guy who does too much to try and impress. He sees how you are and knows what part to play. These guys are infamous in the church. Many of the guys message me on social media because they see my ministry and the things that I do. Sometimes they come too deep. I've met guys who called me their First Lady, said, "God told me you're my wife," and all the other typical preacher pick-up lines. I'm all supportive of a guy who loves the Lord. But, don't be too deep that we can't have fun. Although we're young, there are other topics besides church, scriptures, and prayer.

The last situation I'll talk about is a guy named Andrew. He was a really sweet guy. Like really sweet. He showed me all of the attention. He said the right words. For me, the greatest way to show you care is by words of affirmation. This is something that I learned about myself. I'm not big on receiving gifts. I don't need anyone to do work for me, so it's definitely not acts of service. I can't be around someone too long, so it's definitely not physical touch. But I love when a guy can put together good words, of course, with actions behind them because I've also learned that people just talk. This guy supported my ministry by watching my videos and just giving me words of encouragement to keep going forward. I know it seems unimportant, but it is something that meant a lot to me. So, there were certain points at the beginning where he just kept trying to move too fast. I don't know if it's just my generation. But, it's okay to take things slow. Here's a hint of just too much.

Me: *"Hey. I got busy. Excuse me.* 👆 *"*

Andrew: *"It's no problem at all. I am just getting off from work. Sooo tired. I have been at work since eight this morning, but soon I'll be joining the military. I tuned into your live tonight. Omg, you have no idea how much I needed to hear that! You truly blessed me with that word tonight! You were speaking right to me! I have so much going on, and you made my night so much better♡. I truly thank God for you being in my life! You're an awesome Woman Of God. Keep doing what you're doing. I love it!!"*

Me: *"Oh wow. I am so glad you were encouraged tonight! May God keep and bless you.* 🙏🕊️ *"*

Andrew: *"Amen!! I am so glad I tuned in! And thank you so much! Same for you!!🙏 I know we don't know each other too much, but I feel like I really like you."*

Me: *"Ooh. I thank you so much!"* 😊

Andrew: *"You're welcome!! Also, I can't help but say you are so beautiful, and your personality is like none other. I love it!"* 😊

Me: *"You're too kind. Thank you again! Have a blessed night."* 🙏😊

Andrew: *"No problem at all* 😊 *and alrighty, thank you so much! You have a blessed night as well.* 🙏 *Do you mind if I have your number to text you on?"*

Me: *"Hello. Let's converse through here right now."*

Fast forward, we continued to talk more. I was enjoying the attention and the compliments that he constantly gave me. It was really cute at first. During this time, I was getting a lot of inboxes. This was during 2020, which was the quarantine time, so maybe people were bored, or maybe these guys were already watching and liked what they saw. Whatever it was, I had a lot of DMs. Of course, I didn't reply to all of them because I was so busy and just not interested. He seemed like a nice guy, so I gave him a chance, even though he lived in South Carolina and I lived in New York. You never know what God can do, right? Distance is nothing for God, right? He's a miracle worker, right? The truth is that long-distance isn't for everyone. It takes commitment and a lot of work. When it comes to anything, of course, I go to the Word of God. But, I also go to the internet to look up information. I looked up "Signs you're not cut out for long-distance." One of them was you hate talking on the phone or texting. I'm fine with texting and talking on the phone when it's absolutely necessary, but I prefer to speak to people in person so that I can see facial expressions and body language. FaceTime doesn't give me enough. Secondly, the article says you have trust issues which is not true because God has delivered me from trust issues. I just know that a lot of people are not honest. I feel like having that long-distance causes trust issues in a lot of ways because you may not know the kind of life that person is living in their state. I'm just speaking in my opinion. I hear so many stories about how it works. But, the truth is that you have to do things that work for you. If you feel better in a relationship where you see each other every day, I believe there's no shame in that. And if you're open to the long-distance, that's fine too. One last sign that stood out was if you are a person who gets jealous easily, then it's not for you. I am not a naturally jealous person. I just feel that if someone is with me, they should not be showing any romantic feelings toward anyone else. It's different if it's a business relationship or just a friendship. That's fine and with boundaries. It's very important to have boundaries in friendships with the opposite sex.

But, to continue the story, Andrew was showing the attention I liked, but he was too fast and rushy. It's a red flag if someone wants to rush things. They don't want to go through the process of getting to know you. They just want to reach the end result. Proverbs 19:2, ESV, says, "Desire without knowledge is not good, and whoever makes haste with his feet misses his way." So, I mentioned to him that it was moving too fast. The relationship. Here's the convo.

Me: *"Yes. I have to tell you something. I only see us being friends. I don't want to go past that stage. I hope you can understand."* 😊

Andrew: *"That hurts, but yes, I'll understand."*

Me: *"Would you rather me deceive you?"*

Andrew: *"No, it's fine. I was just hoping and praying we would go the distance. But I guess we're not, sadly."*

Me: *"I'm sorry that you feel this way. However, I feel it's better than me lying and stringing you along."*

Andrew: *"Yeah, I understand. Is there anything I did wrong or something you didn't like about me that made you feel this way?"*

Me: *"No, there's nothing wrong with you. Also, you didn't do anything wrong."*

Andrew: *"Are you sure? Is it because of how far I am from you?"*

Me: *"No, it's not about that. I hope you can understand what I shared with you."*

Andrew: *"Okay, and it's hard, but yes, I understand. I don't want to force anything."*

Me: *"I'm glad you understand."* 😊

Andrew: *"Yes. I understand that."*

That was the end of the conversation. Then he comes back the next day wanting to talk about the situation again.

Andrew: *"Okay, I'm going to be honest. I'm not into the only friends thing. I have always been looking to get to know someone, dating, then marriage. See, the thing is, I'm attracted to you, and that can't just suddenly change, and for me to act like I'm not, I would be lying to both myself and you. I've never really done the friend zone thing. I know we would be great friends, but that's not what I'm into. I'm only looking forward to a future wife."*

Me: *"I understand completely. Although any lasting relationship begins in the friend zone. However, I think it's not best for us to be in a dating relationship. There's nothing wrong with being in a friendship. Again, I hope you can understand."*

Afterward, he replied again to the conversation, and I was just done. I was okay with being friends first. But he wanted to speed. If someone is rushing you to do anything and is unwilling to wait until you're ready, that's a red flag. He seemed a little controlling to me. Like it's nothing wrong with having the mindset of wanting to get married and have a family. God tells us to do it that way. But, it's important to get to know the person before moving forward to a deeper level. Friendship is the start of some of the best long-lasting relationships I know.

Throughout all the stories I told, the purpose is to share the importance of waiting on God to connect you to your life partner. We get hurt and disappointed when we try to do it because we don't obey God and wait for His direction. Don't even focus on finding the one or waiting for the one. Be found doing what you love. That will attract the person. Your light will attract who God has called for you. Sometimes it may attract distractions, but that's when you ask God for discernment. In everything and in every relationship, guard your heart. Be very careful of who you connect to because that person can either pull you from God and your calling or push you into the things of God. It's better to have that person to motivate you in what you were called to do. He knows what type of person suits you best.

8

An Unstable Foundation

I have to be real and say that I dealt with depression in high school and college. I mentioned before about me getting left behind in sixth grade and having to be in the same grade as my sister. That was so embarrassing to me. I felt that God had left me behind. It was an insane experience because I passed every subject with flying colors. So, they put me in AP courses and gave me the honor roll all of the time. I stayed on the dean's list in high school. But, they would not let me go to my correct grade. So, my family moved to Orange County, New York, which is upstate. As my mom and I were in the office with the guidance counselor, we began talking about my educational history. I told her that I was in 10th grade due to getting left behind. She said, "Well, according to your credits, you should be a junior." I was so in shock. But, it was such a blessing, and I was grateful. I was now a junior in the matter of ten minutes of a conversation. We moved upstate at almost the end of the school year like there were like two months left of school. Probably less than that. But, essentially, I skipped junior year. I was so grateful. There was some missed knowledge in my senior year due to not having a junior year. But, thankfully I was able to catch up on studying and learning.

The crazy part was that now my guidance counselors and teachers talked to students about which college we were going to. Everyone had set answers. Some had specific schools that they had already applied to, and others were set in their choice to not go to college. My thoughts were set on going to college. But, I was just beginning the process of finding schools that would be good for me. I started sending in college essays. One college I applied to, Horton College, was a Christian college. I was so interested in going to a Christian college for some reason. I guess mostly because I didn't want to have bad influences around me. But I got accepted. The school was almost five hours away. I also applied to this school, Springfield University, which was four hours away. Both of them were long distances away from home. However, I chose Springfield University because I got accepted and received a four-year scholarship. I thought a four-year scholarship would literally pay for my four years there. I was sadly mistaken. The scholarship went toward helping me pay for this private school tuition. Yes, it was a private school. I should've done deeper research. I was so excited because I had a college to attend and received a scholarship for my academic achievements. I was proud. Then, I received an opportunity to receive three credits if I attended the school for the summer before my first semester started. This was like from July to August. So, it was like a short summer camp. Everyone attended three courses for one credit each course. It was good because I could get some college credits before starting credits. This was my first time living away from home. I had no car. I had no job. My money was running really low. Thank God for my parents sending me money and things that I needed. My aunts also sent me things that I needed. My greatest struggle was not being away from home or not having a lot of money. It was having terrible roommates. Keep in mind that I am Christian. I was raised in a Christian household. So, when I got there, I was like *everyone's coming to learn and get to know people.* I didn't keep in mind the party aspect. That everyone was not a Christian. During that summer, the three Resident Advisors we had named Kim, Keisha, and Samantha, were not good role models at all. The Resident Advisors are supposed to advise how to do things and make sure the rules are followed. They would tell everyone to behave and conduct themselves well around the professors and campus leaders. But, when they weren't looking, they encouraged everyone to drink, dance on each other, and have sex. My roommate, Rachel, was not the best roommate for me to have. She was the type of girl who would play inno-cent and sweet. But, when someone pushed her hard enough, she would fold. She was a follower and wanted to fit in with

81

everyone. I had a problem with her because she would bring this guy to the room and lay in bed with him at night. I would tell her constantly that I was uncomfortable. She got upset and stopped coming to the room unless she needed something. Fast forward, I passed all of my summer classes because I was there to study and do assignments, not mess around or party.

Once the summer was over, I went home. Everyone was then assigned their official roommate for the entire semester. We got paired based on major. I have no idea why else we were paired. But we bumped heads a lot. Her name was Michelle. Michelle had a boyfriend named Steven. Before we went back to campus, we talked on social media about what we would bring to the room that we would be sharing. I brought my refrigerator and microwave. She brought an iron and a fan. Everything was cool at the beginning. I was actually excited about having a different roommate. The issue I had with Michelle was her boyfriend situation. She was the type of girl that needed her boyfriend with her 24/7. Like they literally had to be on top of each other all of the time. This was so annoying. I love the couples that are so secure in themselves and in the relationship that they don't have to be together 24/7. It's important to have your own identity in a relationship. Even though I thought she was too dependent on her boyfriend, I was still nice to her, and we remained cordial. We were friendly, but not friends. I'll explain how my trying to make the "friendship" work stage goes in my life later on. But, as roommates, we established written rules that we both agreed to follow for the room. I was struggling with whether I should go live on campus. My parents didn't think I should go because of the distance. Also, I couldn't drive. So, I was waiting for them to take me. I didn't come on the move-in day. When we got there, we established rules like don't come in too late and interrupt someone's sleep and let the other person know when guests were coming over. There were others. But those were the main ones. Since the beginning of our rooming together, her boyfriend was always there. I was cool with it because she would text and say he was coming. So, I would just leave and do things I needed to do on campus. However, we were unequally yoked as roommates.

"Be ye not unequally yoked together with unbelievers: for what fellowship hath righteousness with unrighteousness? and what communion hath light with darkness?" (2 Corinthians 6:14) This scripture speaks to my whole experience of living with this girl. She was fighting against me just because I wanted her to follow the rules of the room. She didn't think what I thought was inappropriate as inappropriate. There was one mandatory party for all of the students to attend. Kim, Keisha, and Samantha were there, of course. It was going good at first. Everyone was chilling, talking, and getting to know each other. Then, alcohol started to be consumed. Even the RAs were drinking. So, of course, some of the students were following. Everyone then starts grinding on each other. Things started to escalate quickly. Samantha, one of the RAs, comes up to me, pulling to dance. I could smell the alcohol on her breath. She was falling all over the place. I just pulled my arm and went upstairs. My roommate was just enjoying the party when I left. She then messages me, trying to convince me to come back downstairs, saying, "It's cool down here." I was like, "I'm good." I don't judge people who go to parties or whatever. But, for me, it's about the atmosphere. I'm not about being present in the atmosphere of drinking and grinding. That's not my type of atmosphere. There was a short time when she would tell me that her boyfriend was coming over. Then she would stop altogether. I then told her that we had to talk. She never came to the room to talk to me. So, we ended up talking through text messages. We had a long texting conversation. I explained that I was being nice about letting him come over. But, I have to know, and it can't be all of the time. I came to college to study, not hang out with guys. Another concern that I had and told her was about him being in the room and me coming out of the shower or something. Throughout the whole conversation, she disrespected my opinion about the situation. Our conversation became something different when she thought it would be what she wanted.

Me: *"Okay, whatever. I tried to make things better, but obviously, you don't want to."*

Michelle: *"This is not going to be your way. So I'm sorry for you."*

Me: *"And it's not going to be yours, so bye."*

There was much more to the conversation. After a few times of this same occurrence, I reached out to the RA. We went through three mediation meetings. The RA tried to make me not leave the school and agreed with Michelle the whole time. I explained that the issue was that I didn't feel comfortable with her boyfriend constantly in the room, and we've communicated that it's important for her to let me know. She kept saying, "Oh. Tatyana, do you really expect her boyfriend not to come over? I have a boyfriend, and he comes up here to see me all of the time." This girl was a "Christian," going to Christian club and everything. But, she thought it was okay for her boyfriend to be laid up in her bed with her while I was there.

Another thing that annoyed me about the meeting was that she kept telling me, "Oh. You should do the Christian thing." I had told Michelle not to use my little refrigerator in the room anymore. This was because of the disrespect, and I believed I had the right to do what I wanted because it was my property. She thought that was ungodly. I admit I felt bad about telling her to take her things out. But, at the moment, I felt wronged. I think it's good to be a good Christian. But, don't be stepped on or become a pushover. I defended myself in a classy way. This is one of the things that made living away from home difficult. We had two more mediation meetings with that situation, and eventually, nothing changed. But, she decided to leave the room and room with someone else. The residential leaders couldn't find a new roommate for me because everyone had roommates. So, I had a room to myself for my freshmen year.

That was very rare. Students had to specially apply or be in at least junior year to get a single room. I was glad about how that situation turned out. God really worked it in my favor. I was not trying to be on college campus acting up. So many college students leave home goody two shoes, but once they get on campus, they start drinking, having sex, and partying, all the stuff that is sin. So, I stayed away from people who did that and connected to some positive people. Fast forward, I make it through the semester, and I'm registering for courses in the next semester, and it's not going well. I found out that I had a remaining balance for school and that my scholarship was not covering much. I talked to the counselor about different things that I could do. But I just needed money to pay the balance. My parents didn't have it right then, and I don't blame them for not having it. So, I had to go home. This was the onset of my depression for five months.

9

Hanging By A Thread

So, I found out that I could not complete a new semester without paying the balance. I immediately went home. At first, I was optimistic about finding a job to go back to school. I was applying to so many places and was hearing nothing back. My depression really hit at this time. I was so grateful to have graduated from high school and completed one semester of college. But now, it hit me that I had to figure life out. I had no money. No friends. No education to keep me distracted from my inside problems. My family was there as much as they could be. My mom would take me out shopping sometimes, or my dad would give me spiritual advice. I wished there were more for me. I would just sleep and cry constantly. The hurt came from feeling stagnate or not pursuing my goals. I couldn't go to school until I found a job to pay for my balance at school. This was very stressful. I had zero job experience. I believe that's why it was hard. Then I had to go through so many people asking me, "How's school going?" Or "When are you graduating?" This just added to it. Sometimes I would say, "It's fine," because I didn't want the question or the embarrassment of saying I dropped out of school. A lot of people expected more from me. Eventually, I started telling people that I was taking a break. I honestly hated seeing everyone always happy and joking around while I was going through a broken moment. This was the first time that I had suicidal thoughts. I thought things like, "No one cares if I live or die," "It wouldn't matter if I died today," or "What is the purpose of me being here if I don't have a purpose to do anything?" All of these crazy questions were in my mind. Everyone around me was sad for me. I would just cry and mope all day. My dad gave me this stern talk saying, "This has to end today. I can't stand seeing it. God is saying, 'Look at my daughter being defeated.'" I was tired of this state of depression. But, sometimes, you cannot help how you feel. He gave me the task of reading and meditating on one scripture each day. He told me about the power of changing my mindset from negative to positive. I can say some of the things that helped me get out of that everyday cycle of feeling worthless, low, abandoned, defeated, and concerned about my future were finding a home in God.

During this time, I wasn't going on live videos and motivating people to love Jesus like I usually would. I could not even muster up the strength to not sleep all day. I knew I had some work to do. But, that was the thing I was always committed to and excited about. The enemy distracted me that fast. Although I experienced this, I found keys to help in depression are always keeping a positive mindset, talking to godly people, doing things you're passionate about, and always praying and reading God's Word. It took some time for me to step back into that faith mindset. I got back to feeling mentally strong and delivered from depression through a continuous prayer life. I would pray, fast, and read the Bible every day. I knew that this was a spiritual battle. The truth was that I wasn't dealing with the right issue. I was focused on the fact that I had to leave school. But, the real issue was the enemy trying to defeat me. Ephesians 6:12 says, "For we wrestle not against flesh and blood, but against principalities, against powers, against the rulers of the darkness of this world, against spiritual wickedness in high places." Since I have gone through depression myself, I realize that depression is a spirit. It is possible for someone to have a spirit of depression. The enemy was attacking me, and I didn't even know it. The scripture clarifies that we wrestle with principalities. Unfortunately, depression is well known in our world today. Many have been in depression and had been suffering from thoughts of suicide and actually committed suicide. They didn't beat the depression. What stopped my depression was my faith in God and the strength from Him. I also had the desire to be changed and happy. Having faith in God lets me know that no matter what current issue I may be having,

God can help me through it. I also had the Christian mindset to know that people who commit suicide go to hell.

All in all, I had faith that God could and would help me through it. I kept praying and reading my word as a part of my lifestyle. Eventually, I found a job, got hired, and started working. I saved up some money and paid off my school balance. I was then able to apply to another school, and I got accepted. I graduated from that school in the year 2020. I believe I experienced those tough five months to help someone else. If you are going through a moment of discouragement or have lost hope, I encourage you to commit to Jesus. He will comfort you. He will help you know that you can make it through anything. He doesn't care about your past mistakes or your shortcomings. He loves you unconditionally. Through prayer, He will help you through your storm. Your life is worth something. You are important to someone. You are loved by someone. The One that created you created a plan for your life. A good plan that will help you succeed. Never give up. Life is worth living, and you have a purpose for being alive.

10

Supernatural

"For the word of God is living and active, sharper
than any two-edged sword, piercing to the division
of soul and of spirit, of joints and of marrow, and
discerning the thoughts C and intentions of the heart."

HEBREWS 4:12, ESV

My ministry really started back at thirteen when I received Christ. But, I've been doing ministry since fifteen. I didn't get licensed as a minister until 21 years old, not because I couldn't but because it wasn't something that I was pursuing. There are so many young people that are attached to titles in the church but haven't done the work to get the license. In the secular world, if you haven't proven to have a great amount of knowledge and experience about a topic, you're not getting licensed. Now, titles are given too freely in some cases. I did the work for years and then received the license. Since I did it this way, all I had to do was continue doing what I was doing. That's why I don't get how you can be a 17-year-old bishop in Christianity. I don't believe in limiting anyone simply because of their age. However, for me, it's about the level of experience. I have been in ministry speaking the gospel since fifteen. I've been doing the work. So, when I was licensed as a minister, I was always doing the work. And now, today, the title doesn't control me. People are too caught up in being acknowledged by these titles more than focusing on winning souls for Christ. A lot of things need to be back in order in the church. But I digress.

So, I started going back to college, and I was always interested in finding a positive group of people to be around. I eventually found a Christian club on the list of clubs. Unfortunately, it was on the Shineberg campus, and I went to school on the Chester campus. So, that was out of the window. Then I had to move, and the Shineberg campus was closer. I had seen the list of clubs and forgot about the club. But one day, I was walking through campus, and I just sat in this area where this girl was also sitting. We began talking because I asked her, "Is it ok for us to be here?" She was so nice and started talking more deeper. I learned that she was a pastor's daughter. She sang worship at her church with her mom and had a lot of siblings as well. What are the chances of this happening every day? Then she told me about the club, the time it met, and where they met. When I went there for the first club meeting, I was invited to the upcoming leadership meeting. I didn't understand why I was invited because I was new. In the meeting, I was asked to be the club's Vice President. Things escalated quickly because I definitely did not expect the Vice President role. When the President Alexis asked me, she said, " Tatyana, would you mind being my Vice President?" I said, "Yes, because I'm all for spreading Jesus on campus." I just didn't know the responsibility. So, fast forward, the President just stops showing up. She showed me how to do the presentation for the club. But, she just disappeared for a long time. Then I was voted in as President because I was doing the work of the President as a Vice President. It was insane. The group kept trying to get in touch with her, and she was not responding at all. So, I was the new President. I guess you can say I was pushed into leadership. But, I was always doing ministry in my past. I had preached the gospel at many churches and youth services. So, I believe God was preparing me for this time. Weeks went by, and we met a few new people, but they were not consistent in coming. Also, the officers were not coming when they were supposed to even though we had a meeting about availability and scheduled the meetings together. I felt like no one cared about the success of the Christian club besides the club advisors and me because there was a constant excuse of why they could not be there or just not showing up. They would say, "Oh. Class has been a lot, and I have some work to do," or "I have something else planned." Of course, I also had many assignments to do and many other things planned. But I was always there. Eventually, the former President, Alexis, apologized for just leaving the group and said that she would only be there sometimes. I accepted her apology and thought it was good, but I had to step in with little knowledge. One guy, who was the secretary, never came. When we had pizza parties, he was there. I thank God for the girl who invited me and her brother because they did a lot to help me. When we had pizza parties, he was there. We had two meetings, so I dreaded this because they would just show up when they wanted. But we all wanted to give students the option to attend. The prior semester students said they couldn't come because of work or they were in class. So we made sure we had two meeting options. We had posters up, which we made sure were creative. We made the first one as a group. It looked like it would not stand out a lot, so we got a new one done. Shout out to my mother because she helped us out. People noticed the new one more than the other one.

Once that flower was put up, weird things started to happen on campus. There was this satanic group called the Open Circle ⭕ Group on campus. They did not like us because we were spreading Jesus. One day we decided to change our flyer to bright purple. Then they changed their flyer to purple. They began to complain about our outreach. They were basically saying that we were pushing Jesus too hard. I would hear negative comments and get negative looks while walking down the halls. There were a couple of satanic groups there on campus. We would have outreach every other Monday where we would have out bibles, information about the Christian club, pamphlets about Jesus and the principles of Jesus, using cards as witnessing tools, and the Open Circle Group had been experiencing someone posting cards on the Open Circle club flyers. They automatically assumed it was the Christian club. The Student (Bob) Involvement Director sent a complaint to the club mailbox. It said that we were putting things on their flyers or covering them up.

As the president, I asked everyone whether they posted any cards. Everyone said no, and I know I didn't. So I knew it was a lie. The strange thing is that even after all of their complaints about us, they chose to give us a personal invite to a campus event they were having. The group president walked up to us as we were spreading Christ and giving out bibles. She says, "Oh. We're having a spiritual colt night that we want to invite you all to. You can have your bibles and table at the event. There will be other spiritual clubs there as well. I don't discriminate against people's faiths. You know?" We used that moment to talk to her about what they actually believed and what caused her to go that way. She talked about her family, childhood, and everything. She was open to hearing from us. But, the true goal was to invite us to the event. Even though the signs were clear that we shouldn't go, we had meetings and thought maybe it would be good to go into the climate and share the gospel with the lost people. But, through prayer and talking about it, we realized that it was not a good idea to be in that climate simply because of the dangers. We thought about her explanation and how there will be other spiritual groups. If people see a Jesus group, they automatically get defensive or combative. We've experienced that in this time. Also, we had a tabling event elsewhere on the same date. I believe it was an indication from God that we made the right decision. I also started thinking about other things when we decided not to go. I thought, *why would we have to go to this special spiritual colt night to spread the gospel when we're out on campus spreading the gospel already? Couldn't they just come out there?* What is a "colt" night? It seemed wrong. It just seemed like a setup.

In addition to this complaint, one of the Open Circle group members said that they experienced two instances where they were "harassed " by a member of the Christian club. At that time, there was a group called God The Mother, who believed God was a woman. I assumed it was them. They would walk up to people aggressively, force them to take information, and ask personal questions. We would just ask people if they'd like to know about the club. Some would say yes, and others would say no. We would not force them. If they asked for prayer, we prayed for them. If they seemed not interested, we'd say okay and have a blessed day. There were a lot of people I prayed we would see at the meeting because people would say, "Oh, you came to the right person because we're Christians." However, we never saw them at any of the meetings. My heart ached for people who didn't recognize God's power and the name of Jesus. So, the disappointment in seeing some people come to some meetings and not others was that desire to see them be saved and whole through Jesus. However, in the Christian club, we always talked about sowing a seed into someone's life. You might not be that person to convert someone to Christianity then and there. But, guess what that person has heard about Jesus. And when they're going through something that their mom, dad, sister, or friend can't fix, they remember that they can call on Him. I thought that maybe because it was a community college, people had other things to do. However, I remembered how I came to the group, and I actually looked forward to meeting Christians at college. We did not get a lot of people in the group. I was expecting at least twenty people. But, I was thankful for the good ten people we had on the regular. We often received positive encouragement from people.

Once when I was posting flyers, a professor asked if the group had a good turnout or were there a lot of people. I said, "We're just starting this semester's group." She said, "Well, I hope it has a good turnout." That was a moment of encouragement. Another time when we had an open event with free pizza, no one came except the few that sometimes came. After the meeting, two members ran into a group that was talking loudly and gave them pizza and information about the club. From that point on, they were interested in getting involved. I was encouraged a little by that. We were able to get our information posted about the club meetings and events. We had great outreach. Tabling for me was new and sometimes difficult. Usually, the time was 10:30 to 2:30. The club advisor and I would switch off. Like I would do a couple of hours in the beginning and wait until he came toward the end, or sometimes we did it together. It wasn't easy because we were in the lobby, where everyone walked past. So, students in my class saw me standing up for Christianity. My professors saw me out there. Most of them would smile. But, some of them looked down on me, especially my science professor. His facial expressions would be so screwed up. I'll say this, many students who doubted God or had questions would come up and ask. Some people even got more serious about Christ through us being out there sharing our faith publicly.

March 9th was our last outreach because the school closed down due to the coronavirus pandemic. It was a great outreach. People stopped over to play the giant Jenga. We handed out a lot of flyers, and my professor, whom I tried to give the gift, saw the setup. It is nerve-wracking to approach people you don't know, but even worse, being rejected. However, I didn't let rejection stop me. We kept giving out information and playing Jenga with people. The virus shook things up. We could not have the Christian club meetings, and our classes were all switched to online. No one could be on campus anymore. My first thought was that the virus was not as serious as everyone was making it, that it was something minor. But, even though we couldn't meet in person, we made virtual gatherings work for us. It took time for us to share our virtual information with people and set up a virtual presence for the club. But, once we did, we got to meet a lot of new people and talk about Jesus. I am thankful that I could complete the semester and not have to retake any classes because I was in danger of failing math even though I completed all the work and went to all the Zoom meetings. But, because I was also keeping God first, He helped me through my work. He helped me through college because of my commitment to Him. During the shift from in-person to virtual, many people were spreading the pandemic message "20/20 vision." This pandemic was not the 2020 vision people were looking forward to. People also judged prophets who called 2020 the year of 20/20 vision. With many people losing their loved ones, losing jobs, or leaving jobs, battling whether they should be wearing a mask or not wear a mask, whether they should get the vaccine or not get the vaccine, many people were tested, and I believe we still are being tested. I still consider 2020 and even now as a time of being more aware, being able to see through the spiritual eyes. Since I was home during the pandemic, and even though I was busy with school work and other things, I prayed long and hard for the nation. I mean, I have never experienced a pandemic. So, I reached out to God for my group, church, family, and everyone in the world. Even during the Christian club virtual meetings, a girl felt convicted to remove her dream catchers out of her house. She removed the altar that she had created at home. She felt convicted through the Bible studies and scripture that we were sharing. She talked about how she was having nightmares, and then she started to make a change during the Bible Study session. I mean, God was just doing powerful things in this time frame.

During this time, I experienced "sleep paralysis." I was so deep in God's Word and reading a book on the supernatural and angel encounters. I wanted to know about the spiritual world more. At this time, my dreams were getting so clear. I also experienced a heat-like feeling in my right foot and hand. Then my prayer started going to another level. I received the first attack when I spoke a message outside in Harlem, NY, in front of my grandmother's church. My grandmother, a pastor, had a street outreach, and she asked me to have words. She threw me on the spot. It was about a ten-minute message. I mentioned God's forgiveness and that He loves everyone and wants everyone to believe in Him, that He knows the hurts that they have gone through throughout the years and that He can heal their hearts. People were really blessed by the message. Once I went home that night, I was attacked. I was sleeping in my bed, and it was around 3:00 AM when my eyes were open. I was trying to move and could not move. It felt like someone or something was holding me down. I don't know. I was in a panic at first. But then I eventually started calling out Jesus multiple times, and I was able to move after about one minute. I had never gone through that. So, I explained to my family what happened and did my research. They called it "sleep paralysis." But, I was reminded of when I went through the depression and how I learned that it was a spirit. Then I remembered all that I was doing during that time to promote

Jesus. I led the Christian club, my prayer life went up, and I was so deep in Him.

The enemy did not like that, and I was attacked many times. One time, I was sleeping, and I had visions that a dark spirit was standing behind me while I was sleeping. Then another time, I was held down again and heard the enemy say, "Say yes." I said "No," and called Jesus. I believe he wanted me to return to the negative space of addiction and depression. I wouldn't let him win. This was an indication that God was pleased and the enemy was mad. Anything you do for Christ will come with attacks. But, every time I prayed, God delivered me. It just pushed me to go harder with the things for the kingdom. It was so crazy because I was going to class acting fine, and I was fighting a spiritual battle at home. But, you cannot talk to worldly people about spiritual things. So, I would talk to my pastor, who is also my dad, and he let me know that attacks indicated me going higher in God. Proverbs 3:5-6 says, "Trust in the Lord with all your heart and do not lean on your own understanding. In all your ways, acknowledge him, and he will make straight your paths." This scripture brought me through this time. If I leaned onto my own understanding, I would say I couldn't make it and needed to stop because the repercussions of my actions were too great. But, God let me know that I could make it through Him. Because Christ is with you in your situation, you can make it through anything. When you are being tested, it's difficult. It's not easy. But, it makes you stronger, and it teaches you.

Going through these experiences as a Christian leader and going through attacks, I became more aware of the spiritual world. In the world we live in, people believe science is the explanation for many things. When really, it's spiritual. So, the pandemic really was an eye-opener because people or science can really destroy God's creation. God created the world beautifully, and we as a people changed it. I don't believe God caused the pandemic. I believe He allowed us to wake up with people dying left and right, one after the other. I lost my grandmother during the pandemic. She was an awesome woman of God. She had some health issues that have made me want to look out for my health and just make sure I look for some hereditary health issues that I may have. My grandmother lived with my family and me. Her last few weeks were with us. I remember the pain she had. But, I also remember the faith she had in God. Throughout all the pain she had, she kept her faith in God. She always watched gospel shows and listened to gospel music, constantly praying no matter what, going to church when she didn't feel 100%. She was faithful to God. In honor of her memory, I want to be that bold for Christ and have that crazy faith to know that God will be there whatever happens. She always believed in me being a good leader. I remember a time she asked me, "Who's preaching Sunday? You or your dad?" I was shocked when she asked that. I mean, preaching on a Sunday is a major deal. My dad doesn't allow just anyone to preach on Sundays. As the pastor, he usually preaches on Sunday. However, there was a Sunday when my parents went away to Cleveland, Ohio, for a birthday celebration. I had to take my dad's position as the interim leader. It felt good to lead in that capacity. My grandmother was a great woman of God, and I'm surrounded by so many great women of God. My mother, my other grandmother, who is still here, and some of the many women preachers I've met have motivated me to push forward in ministry. The best thing we can do is put our complete trust in God. When I leave here, I want to have security in the fact that I am going to make heaven my home and that I am doing the work that He has called for me to do. We can only make it into heaven by having a relationship with Christ and living a life that reflects Christ. This will cause you to be considered weird in a world where people are all about doing what makes you happy. I've learned that when I obey God, He provides everything I need. He can be my friend when I need Him. He can be my comforter when I need it. Everything that you need, He can be that for you. He can heal that brokenness and take away that hopelessness. This pandemic is one that will turn many people back to Christ. That's the real 20/20 vision when people realize that God is real and that we cannot do anything without Him. God created the world, and He controls it. I will always serve the God who created our world and has been there in my darkest times. God has been my all. That's why I'm so crazy about Him.

11

Can I Even Do This?

"You, therefore, beloved, knowing this beforehand,
take care that you are not carried away with the
error of lawless people and lose your own stability."

2 PETER 3:17, ESV

This scripture is so profound in my life because I have learned that it's not about the quantity of works but the quality of works. A person can be doing a lot of nothing, which means that what one is doing can be pointless in the walk that God has for them to do. It shouldn't be done if it is not a part of God's plan for your life. If it's not a part

105

of God's plan, it's a distraction. If it's not helping you grow, it should not be done. When people are not helping your growth, it's important to let them go. Everything you do should have a purpose. Fortunately, I learned that many things and people are not worth my time and energy. One thing about me is that I love staying busy. But, sometimes, I need to slow myself down. I am a full-time student with a full-time job and also ministering and doing the work in God's kingdom. I promised God that I would continue working in my ministry no matter what He blesses me with. Trying to maintain my ministry is a huge focus of mine. However, I am also big on being educated and having a career that pays you. I know a lot of people with the full-time ministry plan. They think preaching engagements will pay their bills. I have learned from my dad and pastor, who pastors two churches, works a full-time job, and has his own business, that it's important to have your own job and finances in place. I could never even fathom being controlled by a church or an organization to the point where I have to do everything they want me to do or I'll lose my financial stability. So, that's why I go so hard to have a degree and a career. I currently have my associates in social work and am pursuing a bachelor's in social work. I am also working an 8:00 to 4:00 pm job that gives me experience in social work. While also working on this book and speaking at churches. I like having independence and being stable. I drive my own car and make my own money.

My social life has been a little rocky. There's a huge issue of cliques in the church arena. I have experienced disappointment in church people and organizations within the church. In my early teens, this oratorical contest happened every year at the church. There were usually four contestants who had to speak a message on the given topic. The contestants were young people, 13-18-years-old, from different churches in the organization. No other young person wanted to speak. So, I spoke for three years straight. I wasn't expecting to win the contest the first year because I was new to it. The following year, everyone said I got better and was greater than anyone else. But I got third place. The goal of the whole contest was to have the winner speak at the spring rally and win money for school and an award. The last year my church and I were sure that I would win because I practiced more at the church. I even had my aunt, who won one year of the oratorical, help me with my message. I went up to speak that last year. I received great scores and made sure I worked on the things that lost me points last year, like looking down a lot or making this weird noise with my mouth. All of those things changed. Then a girl comes up who didn't have any scripture or didn't even talk about the topic. She instead talked about losing her mom. However, she won, and I got second place. All of this that happened over three years was hurtful. I mustered up enough strength as a young person in the church to go up to speak according to all of these rules, and I was not even given a fair chance of winning because of this competitive spirit in the church. After that, I did no more oratoricals, and the other young people in my church were not motivated to go after me. I always sensed this favoritism in the organization as they would only choose their favorite young people to do something for youth conferences or regular services.

I have also, unfortunately, had some bad experiences when I tried working with other young people in their ministry idea (KPM and Young preachers). This group, "Gods Children," reached out to me about being a part of the leadership team. I was first invited to speak at one of the virtual meetings. It went well, and I gained more followers through that. Then they asked for me to be a part of the leadership team. I started doing Bible studies every week on their page. I was actually not doing videos on my page because it was just a lot to do two live videos on social media while also working and doing school. So, I focused on their movement. The whole time, the group's founder kept trying to get with me. I kept saying this was a business thing, and I did not like him. One day, I looked on the page and noticed that my video had been taken down. To me, that was a slap in the face. I worked so hard for that page, and someone took my video. I reached out to the founder, saying, "Good morning. I posted a live video yesterday for the kingdom talk. The video seems to be gone. Do you know what happened to that video I posted?" I saw that he read and completely ignored it. Honestly, there were a lot of other messed-up things happening. So, I just ended up pulling out of the group. But I did wish them well. When I see signs of shady behavior, I move on. The crazy part is that I was so nice and giving. Then,

I experienced shade from this person. A few months down the line, he hit me up because he saw me driving on the highway. He proceeds to ask me out on a date again. I couldn't believe that he had the guts to ask me out again after the situation that occurred. But I'm not stupid. Once someone shows you how they move, believe them and learn from it.

I had the same experience recently when I was invited to a social media group of young preachers. I introduced myself. Everything was good because the moderators seemed nice and seemed like they generally wanted to get to know other young Christians. But then I saw that cliquish behavior going on again that I talked about before. The thing I hate about being a member of these groups is that your comments are literally controlled. You have to do things according to their way, or it's not right. I operate by being led by the Holy Spirit and the Word of God, not people. When people who are not your pastor try to control you, that's a red flag. I understand why people put restrictions on posts and comments because sometimes people can post crazy things. But, I posted one post during Valentine's Day encouraging all the singles to know that God loved them. Then my post was the only one deleted. It was the same issue with a different person. I then reached out, saying, "Hey. I'm from the new group. Will you clarify what's post-able or not post-able in the group?" She then responds, "Good morning. I pray that you are well, and thank you for being a part. Because we are still growing, we are only allowing introductory posts at this time. Eventually, we will share what will be allowed to be posted." I thought this was a satisfactory response. But then I look on the page and see other posts that have nothing to do with introductions. I didn't reach back out about the issue. I didn't complain or write posts about the group or anything. I just removed myself. The unfortunate truth is that cliques are prominent in the church. But I've learned not to depend on people and trust God because people switch up. Church people are people, people who have bad habits. I could have allowed this feeling of being excluded to pull me out of doing ministry, speaking the gospel, or even going to church. The oratorical could have persuaded me to go the other way and stop speaking the gospel. But, my relationship with God was much greater than any youth competition.

Church hurt. Church hurt is real. Being used for three years for the gain of an organization that I felt didn't really want to give me a chance was hurtful. I could only imagine people who have experienced the same or even worse than I did. Cliques should not be in church. If we want to win souls for Christ, inclusion is the way. Regardless of whether you have a terrible past, have current issues, aren't versed with church mannerisms, or don't know many celebrities in the ministry, you still matter.

Inclusion has to come back into the church where everyone is included and does not feel left out because of favoritism. But, I don't go to church for people. I don't speak the gospel to get rewarded or supported by people. I do it all to please God, who created me to do what I do. I talked about this because I know many people who left the church because of "church hurt." The strength to overcome that is to know that trust cannot be put into people. Your trust should be entirely in God. Psalm 118:8 says, "It is better to trust in the LORD than to put confidence in man." This scripture spoke volumes to me because of what I've gone through with people. I have not gotten to the place where I don't desire friendships. But, I've been very cautious about who I connect with. It helps to have like-minded people to talk to about things sometimes. I have been given an amazing small group of friends to who I can talk to about God and the things I am experiencing. I have two good friends that I talk to almost every day. One of my friends was a member of the Christian club I led. She said, "The club helped me get more serious about God." She's now more connected to God than she has ever been. Another commonality that we have is that she's in the helping field. My other friend, who's 30 years old, has been in ministry a long time and knows a lot and has been through things that I've been through. So, we talk about that and just check in on each other.

The great thing about God is that He's willing and able to provide those like-minded people in your corner to be there for you. It's just a matter of asking for that help in finding those people. Preferably those people that have a similar passion to you. My passion is to help people. That is why I study social work in school and work a job in the social work field. It has not been easy balancing everything. I have had some moments of feeling overwhelmed. I used to read articles in college about students who were also working jobs while in school, and at that time, I didn't have a job. In the session where we read that article, the professor asked those who worked jobs to raise their hand. The majority of the classroom raised their hand. She saw my hand down and said, "I wish I were as lucky as you." I totally laughed it off because I didn't think of it as a profound thing. And at the time, even though I didn't have a job, I was not "lucky" because I was depending on my parents still. But, now, as I work full-time and go to school, I understand the value of working. I never thought I would be working, going to school, and doing ministry all at once. My original plan was to work a social work job and then go to school for my bachelor's later on. However, I didn't want to stop school and not have enough education for my dream career. My dream career has always been in the social work field. However, I just found out that I want to be a case manager. I'm not sure for which population. But, I believe a lot of what I've done in my past and am doing right now prepares me for my dream career.

I remember an internship program experience I had while getting my associate's. Since the coronavirus pandemic came, I was concerned about how my internship with the intern program would continue. *Would I be able to get my hours still? How would the students in the program react to the change? What would happen if I did not reach my forty-eight hours in my internship? Would my graduation goal be set back?* These were all the questions that ran through my mind. I did not want to be held back because of the virus. Some of these questions were results of anxiety about the pandemic mixed with worries about my education. Although it took some time to get back into my internship, the assistant program director met with me to see what schedule would work for me. However, there was a professor who did an awesome job of ensuring that the students had different ways to get the hours we needed. I was even able to explain my concerns about not being able to reach my goal in the program. He gave me many alternatives. However, hosting the student lunch hour caught my interest. The Scout Program student lunch hour is when the student mentors are given the opportunity to socialize with and entertain the Scout Program students. Although there were only two mentors, I and another, we had fun with one another and the students. It was quite different from when we could meet face to face. Even though we could interact with each other, in-person interaction is better. Before the virus outbreak, I never really considered or appreciated the opportunity to meet with peers in person. I have missed being able to hug or even just being close to another person. I appreciated the four hours a week that I had to meet with the students on Google Meet and play games.

As hosts, the other mentor and I would be the ones to keep the students occupied. At first, I was worried about that. I did not know if I could be brave enough to lead something so important. Even though I was the president of the Christian club at Orange County Community College for three semesters and I had to take the lead position, it was different. I had to make sure I chose activities that the students were willing and able to participate in, understanding that the students had specific disabilities that caused them not to comprehend the rules of the games. Since the games had to be virtual, we had some difficulty finding ways to entertain. Nonetheless, we found that teamwork is very important. The other mentor and I created a schedule of what games we would use. We even tried the games with each other to be sure they would work for the students. This was a trial and error thing. We played games like trivia, matching memory cards, numbers games where you have the person guess the number you're thinking, would you rather, person, place or thing, and even truth or dare. It is very different working with people who have disabilities. However, I recognize that they are one of the most overlooked groups of people. This volunteer experience opened my eyes and gave me some tools to be a caseworker today for people with mild disabilities. I cannot share in detail what I do. But, I help people have more fulfilling lives. I love my job.

My job, in a way, reminds me of my ministry. As a minister, I want to help people be encouraged and know that they can make it. If one of my friends needs to talk about life issues, they call me, and we talk about it. And the best thing is that I can do the same. I can call them, and they'll pray for me in my time of need. The crazy thing is my two closest friends are 29 and 30. I've attracted older people in friendships. Maybe it's just how I carry myself and how I think. And there's nothing wrong with that because each person has to go with the type of people that fit their mindset and values. Age is just a number. You may be 20 and come in contact with a 60-year-old woman who's thinking about committing suicide. If you have the words to encourage someone, never feel bound by your age enough to prevent you from saving someone's life, regardless of your age. You can have an impact in this world. 1 Timothy 4:12 says, "Don't let anyone look down on you because you are young, but set an example for the believers in speech, in conduct, in love, in faith, and in purity." You can be the perfect person for that moment. I believe we should all be there for someone to encourage them, even if we're not receiving any immediate reward. Social work and ministry are both selfless areas of work. So, balance is very important. However, social work will always be my passion.

I know I have to balance my work, ministry, and fun. So, now I have been huge on self-care. I go to the movies, hang out with one of my friends, and even watch movies, anything outside of work. Making time for yourself is just as important as my work and education. If I don't get recharged, I know I'll burn out, and I wouldn't be good for helping anyone. I am so grateful for where I am in my life. I used to expect to be married at 22 and living life with "the one." But, instead, I've been doing something even better. I've been doing me, and it feels good. It is empowering to put your complete trust in God. I am grateful that I can have a career that I love, be educated, and work for God. I am in the best place in my life. I know now that, even through the pain, God was always there because I stuck close to Him. One of my favorite scriptures is Proverbs

16:3, "Commit your works to the LORD, and your thoughts will be established."

There have been times when I wanted just to fall asleep rather than complete a paper that was due. There have been many times when I did not want to get up for work in the morning. But, I reminded myself that achieving goals takes work and that hard work eventually pays. I have learned so much through my experiences. Now, I thank God for what I have been through because it made me the strong woman I am today. With so much going on in the world, it's important to stick close to God. Violence has increased. In New York City, perpetrators are going around stabbing people. Immorality has increased. What is perceived as sin in the Bible is acceptable now. A lot of behaviors and practices have become normalized. This doesn't give this generation a fair chance to choose a righteous way of living. Proverbs 14:12, NIV, says, "There is a way that appears to be right, but in the end, it leads to death."

Living according to the Word of God is not something that harms us. It helps us to live longer lives. There may not be a lot of people following righteousness. But, it's still the best. God is not a God of just rules. He is a God of blessings and favor. My career and education goals will never come before maintaining my Christian values. If it questions your values, it's not the right career, group, people, school, or atmosphere. I never want to question or dishonor Jesus Christ to fit in or make it. Never will I get to the point where I sacrifice my Christian beliefs to make it further in my career. God will make a way of success for those who honor Him; that's the beauty of having Him in our lives. He never leaves. We can always turn to Him about anything. Day to day, I represent Christ in several ways. I have stickers on my car about Jesus. I share the love of Christ through how I treat people. We can all be a part of this moment of spreading Christ in the world in unique ways. It's not always about a sermon. Just being there for someone in need is ministry.

Many people sold their souls to satan and the world for riches, worldly success, and recognition. We should not lose our faith and commitment to God and our convictions. Trends should not change us. A standard of holiness is still expected—no matter what law is passed or what becomes right in the sight of government. I want to be a part of the movement to get souls back to Christ – for the world to honor God again. I believe it is possible. It's just about reaching the hearts of people.

I hope that whoever reads this is encouraged by my story. I pray that it motivates you to know that you can manage all the responsibilities on your plate. You can be free from pain, guilt, insecurities, and bad habits. Nothing is impossible through Christ. To that young lady, get that degree, establish a career, or just accomplish some goals, and then the right guy will come to pursue you. It's so important to learn yourself before attaching yourself to anyone else. Be so secure in yourself that if someone chooses to leave or switch up, you're good because you're not dependent upon a person for your happiness. To that young man, know that a woman with more than a pretty face is what you should pursue. A woman that will help you become

117

a better you. But, all in all, find what you need in yourself and in God. I have people in my life that I know I can turn to for prayer or help in general. But, I've learned to be self-sufficient and content with myself because people change.

God doesn't change. However, I'm not blind to the fact that having a companion could be helpful. You'll have someone to confide in daily and just a life partner and friend. And that's perfectly fine because God created marriage for us to enjoy. But, get healed from what's been broken or hurt in you so that when you do find that one that you desire to commit to, you won't punish them for what you've been through in your past. Despite the pandemic we're experiencing, understand that there's much more life ahead. In Christ, there's an abundance of life and peace. Understand that God can still help you succeed in any climate, whether trying to balance school, work, children, or ministry. God is there to give you strength. In Him, your plans will succeed. He'll help you succeed in everything you do when you vow to live a life of discipline and obedience to Him. God has the power to heal your broken heart so that you can feel whole and happy. God expects discipline and a holy lifestyle. He is one who not only gives us another chance; He gives us chance after chance to make it right. His grace and mercy are why I'm still here. He will also help you in those moments when you feel like you're going to fall or are tempted to do wrong. If something is too hard to break off your life, don't be afraid to ask Him. He will make a way of escape. As we increase in degrees and career experience, it's so important to stay in the Word of God. The Word of God is direction. Psalm 119:105 says, "Your word is a lamp for my feet, a light on my path." So, even if you don't know where you want to go next or how you will get there, or even if you are unsure what career fits you, you have all you need when you have God. Trust God, and everything will unfold. Trust God.

REFERENCES

Ambivert. (2022). *Dictionary.Cambridge.org.* Retrieved 6 May 2022 from https://dictionary.cambridge.org/dictionary/english/ambivert.

Etienne, V., Rapaport, L., McPherson, A., Gordon, S., & Derrow, P. (2020, July 22). *Broken Heart Syndrome Spikes Amid Covid-19 Pandemic.* EverydayHealth.com. Retrieved 6 May 2022 from https://www.everyday-health.com/heart-health/broken-heart-syndrome-spikes-amid-covid-19-pandemic/.

Grohol, John M., P. D. (2022, April 28). *Examples of Common Defense Mechanisms.* Psych Central. Retrieved 6 May 2022 from https://psychcentral.com/health/common-defense-mechanisms.

Martin, C. (2016). *Distinctly You: Trading Comparison and Competition for Freedom and Fulfillment.* Bethany House. Pg 132.

McLeod, S. A. (2019, April 10). *Defense mechanisms*. Simply Psychology. www.simplypsychology.org/defense-mechanisms.html.

Overcompensation. (2022). *Merriam-Webster*. Retrieved 6 May 2022 from https://www.merriam-webster.com/dictionary/overcompensation.